Peter the Great

and the Emergence of Russia

Peter the Great
and the Emergence of Russia

B. H. SUMNER, F.B.A.

Warden of All Souls College, Oxford

New York  COLLIER BOOKS

First Collier Books Edition 1962

Third Printing 1965

Peter the Great and the Emergence of Russia *was published
in a hardcover edition by The Macmillan Company.*

*This title first appeared as a volume in the Teach Yourself
History series under the general editorship of A. L. Rowse*

The Macmillan Company, New York

PRINTED IN THE UNITED STATES OF AMERICA

Contents

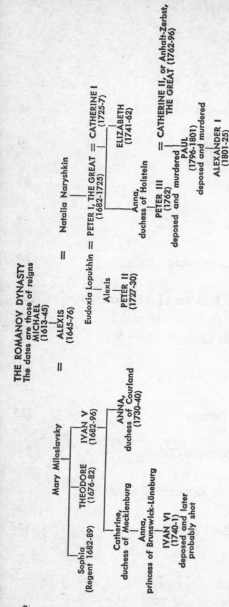

THE ROMANOV DYNASTY
The dates are those of reigns

MICHAEL
(1613-45)

ALEXIS
(1645-76)

= Mary Miloslavsky

= Natalia Naryshkin

Sophia
(Regent 1682-89)

THEODORE
(1676-82)

IVAN V
(1682-96)

ANNA, duchess of Courland
(1730-40)

Catherine, duchess of Mecklenburg

Anna, princess of Brunswick-Lüneburg

IVAN VI
(1740-1)
deposed and later probably shot

Eudoxia Lopukhin = PETER I, THE GREAT = CATHERINE I
(1682-1725)   (1725-7)

Alexis

PETER II
(1727-30)

ELIZABETH
(1741-62)

Anna, duchess of Holstein

PETER III
(1762)
deposed and murdered

= CATHERINE II, or Anhalt-Zerbst,
THE GREAT (1762-96)

PAUL
(1796-1801)
deposed and murdered

ALEXANDER I
(1801-25)

NICHOLAS I
(1825-55)

ALEXANDER II
(1855-81)
assassinated

ALEXANDER III
(1881-94)

NICHOLAS II
(1894-1917)
abdicated and later murdered

6

Peter the Great

and the Emergence of Russia

Chapter 1

Peter I, Tsar of Muscovy

IN THE COURSE of the last two and a half centuries four countries have emerged as newcomers of the first rank in the arena of world history—Russia, the United States, Germany, and Japan. The Germany of Bismarck and Hitler, which was built up on the Prussia of Frederick the Great, is for the time being a dismembered wreck, its future shape and spirit a dark and ominous riddle. Japan, after a bare eighty years of "westernization," at present lies almost prone. Russia, after two hundred and fifty years of "westernization," to-day divides and permeates the world in rivalry with the United States. Certainly no historical theme is for us more significant than the double transformation that has taken place—of Muscovy into Russia and of Russia into the Soviet Union, a transformation linked indissolubly both by contemporaries and by posterity with the names of Peter the Great and Lenin.[1]

Mr. A. L. Rowse has written: "No one can deny that, within limits, the action of a great man at a critical stage may be decisive." Lenin was presented with his chance in 1917; "he was prepared for it and knew how to use it."[2] Somewhat similarly, though on a smaller and less profound scale, Peter the Great was decisive in the long process of transforming medieval Muscovy into modern Russia and in her emergence as a state of the first consequence for the history both of Europe and Asia. In the hundred years preceding the French Revolution, four rulers stand out as epitomizing the age of enlightened despotism—Louis XIV, Peter the Great, Frederick the Great, and Catherine the Great. The fact that two of

[1] See in this series *Lenin and the Russian Revolution*, by Christopher Hill.

[2] *The Use of History*, p. 211.

those monarchs are Russian is striking testimony to the new entrant into the European family of nations. At the cost of over-simplified exaggeration it may be said that it was Peter the Great who revolutionized both Russia and, ultimately, Europe by forcing Russia into the western world.

Peter was born in 1672,[3] and died in 1725 at the age of fifty-two. He ascended the throne when a small boy in 1682, as joint tsar with his elder half-brother Ivan V, but he did not himself assume power until 1695, when he was twenty-three. Thereafter, for thirty whirlwind years he was in actuality as well as in title sovereign, a tsar such as Muscovy never experienced before and an emperor such as Russia never experienced since.

More than half his life belonged chronologically to the seventeenth century. If a great man is a creator of a new age—and all agree that Peter's reign marks something of a dividing line in Russian history—he is also the creature of his own age. Peter grew (explosively) out of seventeenth-century Muscovy, which was far removed from seventeenth-century Europe. Most of the reforms that he carried through linked on with tentative steps in the same direction made by his predecessors; most of the changes that he introduced had their harbingers before him. The dæmonic element in Peter's personality, his violence and cruelty, the unrelenting pace that he set, the magnitude of the ubiquitous burdens that he imposed—these features of his reign have given the impression that Peter broke completely with the past, and that the period of imperial Petrine Russia, which lasted until the October Revolution, was sundered by a broad, unbridged chasm from the period of Muscovite tsardom, which had begun to take shape in the late fifteenth century. It was not so. The

---

[3] All dates are given in the New Style, i.e. according to our present Gregorian Calendar, brought into use by Pope Gregory XIII in 1582. In Peter's day Russia, like England until 1752, used the Old Style, i.e. the Julian Calendar, brought into use by Julius Cæsar, which was then eleven days behind the New Style. Russia did not adopt the New Style until 1917.

greatness of Peter lies in the fact that to a large extent he gave shape to needs and aspirations growing within Muscovite society of the late seventeenth century.

What was this Muscovy in which Peter was born and over which he was to reign? Though very large in size, it was far smaller than what we are accustomed to think of as Russia. It was centred on Moscow and the Volga, reaching down that great artery to Astrakhan at its mouth on the Caspian. Like Astrakhan, the middle Volga region, comprising the old Moslem khanate of Kazan, had been conquered by Ivan the Terrible in the middle of the sixteenth century. Thereby Muscovy had begun that eastward expansion and absorption of non-Russian, non-Christian peoples which have been so predominant a feature in the Russian empire. Within a century of Ivan, the Urals had been engulfed and the immense, largely uninhabited stretches of Siberia added to the Muscovite dominions. With indomitable hardihood the Russian version of the *conquistadores* had even penetrated to the Pacific ocean and established on its shores a few bleak settlements. Northwards the old Muscovy stretched to the White Sea, where Archangel, icebound for half the year, was its one direct outlet to western Europe. From the Gulf of Finland and the Baltic it was cut off by the possessions of Sweden.

On the west, Peter's father Alexis had only very recently reconquered from Poland Smolensk, the noted fortress town a hundred and fifty miles from Moscow on the main route to the West. At the same time Alexis had won from Poland the great prize of Kiev, the cradle of Russian Christianity and the early medieval capital, as well as that part of the fertile Ukraine lying on the left bank of the Dnieper. Colonization was spreading steadily southwards over the black-earth steppes, but the limits of regular settlement were still three to four hundred miles from the Black Sea. The intervening debatable lands were the grazing and hunting-grounds of the Crimean Tatars, subject to the Ottoman sultans, who were largely dependent for their livelihood on raiding Muscovy and the Ukraine for prisoners and stock. They were matched by the semi-independent Cossacks of the Dnieper[4] and the Don, unruly but adept frontiersmen and irregular cavalry.

Though huge in mere extent, vast tracts of which were forest or tundra, the Muscovite empire was very thinly populated. Besides Russians, many different peoples, mostly Moslem by religion, owed allegiance to "the Great White Tsar," but the Russians dominated in numbers and were wholly predominant in government and power. The population may be very roughly estimated in 1680 at perhaps about eight millions. If so, it was probably about equal to that of Poland, but about three times larger than that of Sweden (including her Baltic possessions); much larger than that of England and Wales (about 5,500,000), but more than twice as small as that of France.

It was said by a contemporary of tsar Alexis, in words that sum up the prevailing attitude of his subjects: "Thou, O Tsar, dost hold in thy hands the miraculous staff of Moses, with which thou art able to work marvellous wonders in government. In thy hands there is full autocracy."[5] It was said by a nineteenth-century Russian historian that in the conditions of Muscovy centralization of government was necessary, like "a surgical bandage on a sick limb suffering from bad circulation and lack of internal cohesion." The bandage became a strait-jacket, and already in the later seventeenth century a Russian official was always kept in leading strings; he was never trusted and the slightest independence was feared; therefore "he was kept, like a child, swaddled in long, meticulous edicts, and on each new unforeseen occasion the grown child asked for instructions." So Peter, to his disgust, was only too often to find.

In fact, only a wholly exceptional ruler could wield

---

[4] These Dnieper Cossacks were known as Zaporozhian, i.e. beyond the cataracts of the Dnieper, where they had their fortified camp, near Catherine the Great's foundation Ekaterinoslav, now renamed Dniepropetrovsk, and near to the great Dnieperstroi hydro-electric plant.

[5] Unless otherwise stated, all quotations are from Peter's letters, etc., or from other contemporary sources.

the plenitude of power that in theory was his. Legislation was still promulgated under the old formula "the tsar has decreed and the magnates have assented," but by the close of the century the council of magnates had decayed, and its place was being taken by a fluctuating inner ring of close counsellors of the tsar. These included some individuals from the old aristocracy, but usually the main influence was wielded by his favourites and permanent officials, most of them drawn from the middling or small landowners. Personal absolutism functioned less through aristocratic than through bureaucratic channels. Government by a centralized, but ill-designed and ill-controlled, bureaucracy was already well on its way during the boyhood of Peter.

There had grown up in haphazard fashion thirty to forty departments of state, with their dependent officials in the provinces. Projects for departmental reform were in the air: some regrouping was effected, and Alexis attempted to concentrate control in a new "department of secret affairs." Projects for administrative reform, especially in the ever-pressing realm of finance, were under discussion. The land tax, assessed on a bewilderingly complex basis, was changed for a tax on households (1681). At the same time, other direct taxes were simplified. State monopolies covered a wider and wider variety of goods. More and more money was needed, but deficits continued the rule. Though the taxes (with certain exceptions) were not farmed, the traditional Russian attitude to service as a means of enrichment persisted, with all its consequences of bribery and embezzlement. This was the most damaging of what was styled by Alexis "the evil-designing Muscovite customs," in attempting to root out which Peter was to expend untold labours.

Justice was in the hands partly of officials in Moscow, partly of sheriffs appointed throughout the country by the government. The sheriffs combined with justice not only a host of administrative duties but military functions as well. Muscovite rule, compounded both of brutal punishment and of dilatory complexity, was severe and drastic. Banditry was endemic and violent crime a commonplace.

The block and the gallows, impalement and quartering, mutilation, branding, and the knout, hard labour in Siberia —these equally were commonplaces. The ruler did not fail to strike hard on occasion against the high as well as the low. Princes and noblemen might be tortured and knouted, exiled to the far north, or in extreme cases executed. All classes were liable to drastic punishment and violent exactions. "My mother whips me, and I whip the top"—Muscovy bore grim witness to the truth in this adage.

While autocracy functioned to a growing extent through bureaucracy, it continued to have as its basis the landed interest. This meant the serf-owners, of whom the tsar himself was the biggest. They ranged from the magnates, with a thousand or several thousand serf households (the handful of old princely families and the "new rich" who had been heavily endowed by the Romanov dynasty), through the middling landowners to the impoverished backwoodsmen and the small men of service in the army or government employ. Many held land for life only in return for service, but this form of tenure was in fact, though not yet in law, becoming converted into hereditary possession. The important divisions between the land-owners were not those of legal title, but of birth and wealth. The ties of the family were still powerful in all ranks of Russian society, not least among the landed class. The individual rarely stood alone. Family honour and family interest were paramount.

At the summit of society this clan spirit, as it may almost be called, was enshrined in the elaborate system of precedence which strictly regulated the holding of offices and frustrated the rise of talent both from inside and outside the aristocracy. Its numbing effects had been for long recognized, and most of the military campaigns of Alexis and his father Michael had had to be fought "without precedence." In 1682, a few months before Peter's accession, a far-reaching reform was carried out, when the record books were publicly burnt and the strangling custom of precedence was solemnly declared abolished. Thereby the worst effects of inordinate family pride and of bitter rivalry among the aristocracy were removed; but it took many years, as Peter was to become well aware, before the habits of mind associated with the code of precedence could be outlived.

In the current language of that day the subjects of the tsar fell into two classes—they were either "orphans" or "slaves." The latter were the serf-owners, the former the rest of his people. Peter objected as strongly to his nobles addressing him as his "slaves" as he did to their physical prostrations before his presence. Both customs were indicative of the lack of self-reliance, the backwardness of social development, and the grovelling obsequiousness that characterized so much of Muscovite life. As the serf-owners behaved towards their lord and master the tsar, so should the serfs behave to their immediate masters the serf-owners. Peter himself referred to the serfs as "subjects" of their masters. The mentality bred of serfdom not only kept the serfs in chains but their owners in chains to the sovereign.

Serfdom was the basis of Muscovy and the greatest impediment to productive change. The overwhelming majority of the population were peasants, and of these the greater number were serfs of various types, bound to the land or to their masters, some owing labour service, others paying dues in produce or money. Their condition and methods of agriculture, broadly speaking, were those of the serfs of medieval Europe. Throughout the seventeenth century the power of the middling and smaller landowners was growing, for on them the state largely relied for onerous military and civil duties. Hence, in their interest, the Code of Laws issued in 1649 under Peter's father Alexis reinforced and extended the bonds of serfdom. Slavery still existed in certain legal forms, but was not a dominant element in the social structure of Muscovy. In addition, there were various other classes of peasants, some on the borderline of serfdom, others small freeholders, others semi-military colonists. There were also many casual labourers, vagrants, and nondescripts who escaped being fitted into the bureaucratic stratification of classes which the central government, ever in quest of taxes and services, struggled to impose on a thinly spread and in part fluid population.

The dominant feature of the social structure of Muscovy proper was serfdom, but a far more variegated pattern was characteristic of the "frontier" to the east and the south. This was a magnet for all types of runaways from the thrall of services and dues. The lands of the Don Cossacks especially were a traditional refuge for escape from the long arm of Moscow, more and more pertinacious in seeking control of the "frontier" and in rounding up fugitive serfs and men of service. It was a Don Cossack, Stenka Razin, who raised the standard of revolt and set in flames all the Don and the Volga as far as Kazan; "bandit, outcast from God and traitor" in the eyes of the loyal, but "bold champion of the good," with a halo of legendary prowess by land and sea, in the eyes of the shifting, underdog world of the Volga and south-eastern steppes.

The revolt of Stenka Razin, like previous and subsequent peasant revolts, was essentially an unorganized social uprising, without a political programme. His manifestos had as their watchword "for the Lord Sovereign and the populace." It is typical that there was rumoured to be with him the tsarevich (who actually had just died). His aims were simple and naked. "We wanted to take Moscow, and to thrash to death all you magnates and landowners and the government men." Autocracy was challenged in its underlings, not specifically in itself. It took two full years of civil war before the Muscovite army could smash the rebellion (1670–2). Despite drastic repression the "frontier" remained a powder-barrel, as Peter learnt to his cost.

Towns were very heterogeneous in social composition, and they were small, with the exception of Moscow, "outside a spendid Jerusalem, inside a poor Bethlehem." Townsfolk, for the most part, were freemen in the sense that they were not bound like the serfs to their masters, but they were hampered and curbed by a host of regulations, and their restlessness under heavy taxation and the contemptuous arbitrariness of the local authorities frequently took violent shape in rioting. Locally elected bodies, which earlier had played a considerable part in administration and justice, had almost completely atrophied by the latter part of the seventeenth century, just as the national assembly of the land, analogous to the estates general in western countries, failed to perpetuate itself and no longer met in regularly constituted session after 1653.

None the less, the merchants and traders, very small in actual numbers and despised though they were by the dominant land-owning class, were gaining in importance. The greater part of the taxes were paid by or levied in the towns. The merchants, organized by the state in two guilds, were indispensable in government finance. Though local self-sufficiency was very prominent, a national market was developing. Internal excise duties were being simplified; the great fairs were spreading their influence wider. Handicrafts and small-scale industry were expanding. There was much skilled workmanship and considerable specialization. Metallurgy on an increased scale was developing, partly under foreign direction, but the vital needs of the army could not be met either in quantity or quality from home production.

Hides, flax, and hemp—the two latter staple articles of export—were worked up, and Russian leather goods were already known in foreign markets; Russian furs, a mainstay for state profits, were still better known. Tar, pitch, and other lumber products, together with potash, tallow, and wax, likewise contributed largely to exports. In exchange Muscovy imported a variety of luxury goods, but also munitions, woollens, and many miscellaneous items, such as pins and needles, "German caps," and other harbingers of spreading western influence. In addition, foreign specie was especially sought after by the government, as in most western countries of that day. Muscovy was short of precious metals, and her coinage was both depreciated and insufficient in quantity.

External trade was closely controlled by the state and was mainly in the hands of foreigners operating through Archangel. The discovery of the White Sea route by Chancellor in 1553 led to commercial penetration by

English and Dutch merchants, originally in rivalry for the transit trade in Persian silk rather than for Russian goods themselves. The trade route from Archangel to Moscow, mostly by water, became a main artery, and these northern regions, lying far removed from the depredation of wars or Tatar raids, were studded with flourishing communities. In contrast, the earlier developed connections with the West through Novgorod and Pskov to the Baltic, though still of consequence, had diminished in importance. The foreigners had always been opposed by the Muscovite merchants, who accused them of "having made naked the Russian land," and under Alexis their privileges were severely reduced, to the monopolistic advantage of the small clique of big-scale Muscovite merchants (1667).

On the outskirts of Moscow, the so-called "German suburb" was the centre for the foreigners: merchants, men of diverse trades, doctors, and, above all, military men. Ever since the sixteenth century western engineers, gunners, and mercenaries had been employed in Muscovy. By the time of Peter's boyhood there may have been some three thousand foreigners in all in Muscovy. Almost entirely Protestant, for the most part Dutchmen, Germans, English, or Scots, they were in the main a rough lot, adventurers or soldiers of fortune, but their style of living and their range of knowledge brought a gust of air from the busy, methodical, inventive West that went not only to Peter's lungs but to his head.

In this variegated, growing Muscovy, rich in resources which were as yet either untapped or little developed, the great mass of the population were largely self-sufficient, materially and spiritually. They felt no need for the West, and despised or feared foreigners. Xenophobia was fostered by exaggerated nationalism, born of ignorance, religion, and pride in the centuries' old struggle against the Catholic Poles and the Moslem Tatars. Most of the upper class shared the same feelings, and it was a common observation of foreigners visiting Muscovy that no people had such an unreasoning pride in themselves and their country. In contrast with this self-sufficiency of the multitude, there was a growing realization in governing circles that Muscovy was in certain ways backward in comparison with European countries, especially in military matters, in wealth, and in education, and that she required to borrow from the West if she were to develop the strength to succeed in her pressing problems in foreign affairs.

Military needs, above all, had necessitated the hiring of foreigners, and had emphasized dependence on trade and contact with the West. Bitter experience had proved how ineffectual the army usually was in any prolonged operations or in an offensive campaign. By Peter's time the old-fashioned cavalry, furnished and led by the nobles and landowners, was the deserved butt of scathing criticism. The streltsy, part palace guard, part standing army and police force, organized in twenty-two regiments each about a thousand strong and stationed mainly in Moscow, were more addicted to armed outbursts than fitted for serious military operations. Peter was to have good reason to regard this Muscovite version of the janissaries with special loathing and fear. They were a hereditary, privileged force, recruited for the most part from the townsfolk, partly engaged in trade and handicrafts, living apart in their own quarters, an incitable hotbed of superstition, pride, reaction, and religious dissent.

The effective core of the army was represented by what were called "the troops of foreign formation," or "soldier regiments." These were armed with muskets and officered and trained by westerners, though not yet enrolled as a permanent force in peace-time as well as during war. The first such troops had been organized on a small scale half a century earlier, had owed much to the roving military adventurers supplied by the Thirty Years' War. By the sixteen-eighties out of a total muster of 164,000, these new-fashioned infantry and cavalry regiments, together with artillery, comprised 89,000.

Western influences were also becoming marked in some circles of the aristocracy and the government. Foreign diplomats were increasingly frequent and contacts with them increasingly close. A species of post was introduced from Moscow to the West. The court itself, for all its interminable, religious ritual, was not sealed from the new currents. The young children of Alexis were taught Polish and Latin. Plays were occasionally performed by German actors. Literature was beginning to borrow from the West. Translated books were on the increase. Tsar Alexis at the very end of his reign, reversing his own previous tendencies to innovation, issued an edict penalizing the use of foreign dress and the practice of shaving beards. None the less, such newfangled customs were not stamped out. On the contrary, tsar Theodore revoked his father's edict, and novelties were so rife that some years later the patriarch had to repeat his fulminations against cosmetics, tobacco, foreign hairdressing styles, and especially against imitating "pagans and heretics, Lutherans and Poles" in shaving the beard: man was made in the image of God with a beard, not like cats, dogs, or monkeys.

More important, though for the people at large less evident, western culture was beginning to affect education, partly through direct contact with Europeans and European books, partly through influences from the Ukraine, where the Kiev academy and the struggle against Uniates[6] and Jesuits had fostered the study of Latin and the combating of Catholics with their own intellectual arms. Among Alexis' most trusted counsellors there was a little group of far-seeing, educated men alive to the value of western learning, possessing western books, and prepared for innovations. Peter's half-sister, the regent Sofia, had as her lover and principal minister a man of the same stamp, prince Basil Golitsyn, a scion of one of the greatest aristocratic houses. He was conspicuously ineffective in action, but he delighted in talk of far-reaching reforms. These included the education of Russians abroad and the employment of foreign teachers in Russia, reforms in the army, reforms in serfdom, and religious toleration. There was a new stirring in that stiff and circumscribed Musco-

---

[6] The Uniate Church had been created in Poland in 1596 as a means of winning over the Orthodox to Rome. It acknowledged the Pope, but was allowed to keep its own liturgy and rites.

vite world, a western breeze which Peter from his earliest days imbibed with relish.

All foreigners agreed that ignorance was the besetting weakness of Muscovy. It was not merely that the great bulk of the population was illiterate. That was true of most European countries of the time. To a large extent cut off from the West as a result of the Mongol conquest in the thirteenth century, having always drawn upon Byzantium, not Rome, for culture and learning, Muscovy had remained almost untouched by the four great developments that had made a new Europe between 1400 and 1700—the Renaissance, the Reformation, the Discoveries, and the Scientific Spirit.

The need for education was recognized by some Russians themselves as an urgent task, but what form it should take continued a battleground between the "Greeks" and the "Latins." The fight largely centred on a new academy set up in Moscow in imitation of that in Kiev. If Constantinople had been able to supply genuine and able teachers, the "Greeks" might have won the day, but the failure to do so resulted in thirty years of confused wrangling from which little emerged save a decline in the general repute of Greek culture and a heightening of that of Ukrainian. The way lay open to increasing Ukrainian influences in the church, which spelt both increased literacy and better training of the clergy and an element of secular education.

The divisions within the Church on education were all the more weakening in that they coincided in time with the great Schism which rent in twain the Orthodox, Muscovite "Third Rome." The culture, education, and outlook of Muscovy had been dominated by the Orthodox church. Identified with patriotism and defence against the Mussulman East and the Catholic West, the church, headed by the patriarch, shared with the tsar paramount power throughout the land. In 1667 a Church Council in Moscow, attended by all the patriarchs of the Orthodox churches in person or by deputy, anathematized the Old Believers; that is to say, those who refused to accept the reforms and changes in ritual and liturgy introduced during the previous fifteen years under the leadership of the ardent but overbearing and autocratic patriarch Nikon. He himself, after having been for some years all-powerful with tsar Alexis, arrogated to himself the position of "Lord Sovereign," insisted upon the inviolability of ecclesiastical lands and jurisdiction, and quarrelled violently with Alexis. He was condemned by the Church Council in 1666 and deprived of his position as patriarch. The consequences of this struggle between the claims of the church and the state were important in Peter's dealings with the church, but the contemporaneous and intertwined struggle with the Old Believers has an even greater place in Russian history.

The essence of the Schism was that a large section of the Russian people refused to accept the changes introduced in ritual and the corrections made in the liturgy. These were repudiated as "Greek innovations." They clung to the outward forms of religion in which for them was symbolized the faith of their fathers, the pure salvation of Orthodoxy, the treasured and unique possession of their own, national church, for two hundred years the one remaining rock against Turks and Romans. Ever since the days of Ivan the Great and Ivan the Terrible, the Russian people had been taught to believe that they alone possessed the true, uncontaminated faith, enshrined in sacrosanct texts and rites. Now they were told that their texts were corrupt and must be corrected in the light of the Greek originals, that their ritual did not correspond with that of the fountain-head of Orthodoxy, Byzantium, and must be changed accordingly. They would not abandon what was to them old, though in fact it was the work of the sixteenth century, and would not tolerate what was to them new and foreign, though in fact these "Greek innovations" had much the better claim to antiquity.

Thus, the Old Believers stood out against everything that was non-Muscovite, against all novelties, against the growing, westernizing tendency in the governing circles in the second half of the seventeenth century. Though all the bishops and most of the upper clergy were ranged against them, they had during the first generation (but not subsequently) many supporters among the upper class, and their adherents remained numerous among the trading class, the independent peasantry, the streltsy, and the Cossacks.

At the same time, they included many of the most active and deeply religious spirits of the age, most notably their steadfast and heroic leader Avvakum.[7] He himself was burnt (1682), and the secular authorities gave every assistance to the ecclesiastical. Persecution did but intensify the opposition of the Old Believers. On the shores of the White Sea, the Solovetsky monastery formed a nucleus of armed resistance for all and sundry against the government, and held out for seven years before the government troops won the day (1669–76). Already the development that was to cause such concern to Peter and his successors had begun. The schismatics found support and breeding-ground far and wide among the unprivileged. Opposition on religious grounds to the state and the official church became merged with opposition on economic and social grounds. "All in Moscow is according to the will of the magnates. What the magnates wish, that they do." Such was the very representative summing-up of one determined schismatic sent into exile in the remotest corner of Siberia.

Persecution, often in the most brutal forms, had the effect of fanning the extremes of religious exaltation. These went to the length of self-immolation by fire. Between 1684 and 1690 some twenty thousand saved their souls by sacrificing themselves in the flames of funeral pyres. The more general attitude among the Old Believers was that of suffering endurance, often combined with withdrawal into the "wilderness" or "the frontier," and with belief in the reign of Anti-Christ. The fact that the state backed up the church in enforcing the reforms resulted in the Old Believers being alienated as much from the tsar as from the patriarch. This had the very unpleasant consequence that the tsar could be identified with

[7] There is a translation of his very remarkable autobiography by Jane Harrison and Hope Mirlees (London, 1924).

Anti-Christ. Already, before Peter was born, his father was thus branded.

Such were the profound religious and cultural cleavages, the hopes and fears, the superstition and ignorance, with which Peter had to reckon. He himself experienced only too searingly during his early years some of the darkest sides of Muscovite life, and in escape threw himself with abandoned zest into what was repugnant to the mass of his subjects.

Born in 1672, Peter was the fourteenth child of his father, but the first of his mother, Natalia Naryshkin, the second wife of tsar Alexis. This second marriage aroused considerable opposition. The Naryshkins were an unknown country family, and they now displaced at court the adherents of the tsar's first wife, Mary Miloslavsky. Of her children six daughters and two sons were living. Both these boys, Theodore and Ivan, were sickly and ailing, whereas Peter grew up strong, healthy, and precociously alive.

We have a glimpse of him as a child of three in a court procession. "Immediately after the coach of the Tsar there appeared from another gate of the palace the coach of the Tsaritsa. In front went the chamberlains with two hundred runners, after which twelve tall snow-white horses, caparisoned with silk, drew the coach of the Tsaritsa. Then followed the small coach of the youngest prince, inset with golden ornament, drawn by four diminutive ponies, with four dwarfs riding at the side, and another dwarf behind." The tiny coach, an exquisite piece of foreign workmanship, is still to be seen in Moscow. It was the gift of Natalia's foster-father, one of the tsar's most trusted counsellors and a lover of western innovations, who had married a Scottish lady, an aunt of Natalia.

The chances seemed that both Theodore and Ivan would die in youth, leaving her son the heir. It proved otherwise, and the succession question was to be as important in Peter's early life as it proved to be in his closing years. Suddenly in 1676 Alexis died, when only forty-seven, and Theodore succeeded. The rivalry between the step-mother and the step-children and their adherents gathered strength. Natalia and Peter were pushed into the background of the Kremlin quarters, and her family supporters were ousted from their offices. Six years later Theodore died childless, and Peter at the age of ten (1682) was plunged into a haunting nightmare of mutiny and bloody struggle for the throne.

There was no definite succession law, but if normal custom were followed, Ivan, who was six years older than Peter, would become tsar. Ivan, however, was nearly blind, had difficulty in speaking, and was subject to some form of epilepsy. In either case a regency would be necessary. If Peter were tsar, his mother would be regent, and power would pass to the numerous Naryshkin clan; if Ivan, their rivals the Miloslavskys and their supporters would gain the day, with Ivan's sister Sophia as regent. Sophia was an exception among the females of the royal family. Squat and uncomely, looking forty when she was but twenty-five, she had been brought up with some tincture of western education and was "a princess of a masculine spirit, unlimited ambition, and great parts."

At first Peter was proclaimed tsar, though with considerable division of opinion. A fortnight later the streltsy, worked upon by various genuine grievances and by the wildest rumours, ran riot and invaded the Kremlin. For three successive days the state rooms, private apartments, and even the churches in the Kremlin were a prey to the drunken soldiery clamouring for the blood of the Naryshkin party. Ivan had to be brought out on to the steps of the Red Staircase hand in hand with Peter and his mother to convince the streltsy, milling right up against the two boys, that he was alive. A dozen and more of the leading nobles and the Naryshkins were done to death, stabbed with halberds. Their bodies were thrown out into the courtyards and hacked in pieces.

After these ghastly scenes of mob brutality, Ivan and Peter were proclaimed joint tsars and Sophia regent. Peter's adherents were either killed, in hiding, or exiled. The Miloslavskys triumphed. But the streltsy had gone beyond all limits. Sophia after a few troubled months succeeded in curbing their worst pretensions, and she was strong enough to execute summarily their braggart commander, prince Khovansky. At the same time she defied his insurgent protégés the Old Believers, who had a strong following among the streltsy, and proceeded to launch a new wave of persecution against them.

The regency of Sophia lasted for seven years (1682–9), while Peter was growing from boyhood to adolescence. He continued to live much of the year in the ill-omened Kremlin, appearing with Ivan on numerous ceremonial occasions, surrounded with all the wearisome pomp and long-drawn-out ritual that embalmed the majesty of the successors of the Byzantine emperors. In contrast with Ivan's all-too-apparent debility, foreign envoys remarked on Peter's forward liveliness and sharp eyes: "a youth of great expectancy, prudence and vigour"; "his stature is great and his mien is fine . . . he has such a strong preference for military pursuits that when he comes of age [he was at that time only twelve] we may surely expect from him brave actions and heroic deeds." Apart from official audiences and religious ceremonies, he was left in the background with his mother and various tutors, escaping during the summer months to longer and longer sojourns in one or other of the royal residences in the neighbourhood of Moscow.

Like almost all little boys, he had a great partiality in his toys for soldiers, cannon, and bows and arrows; also for drums and trumpets and cymbals. Like most little boys in rude health, he liked making a noise and being thoroughly boisterous. What is remarkable in Peter is that this infantile partiality developed into a boyish passion for weapons and tools and military games, and from that into the lifelong absorption of the grown man in all things military and mechanical. Throughout his life he delighted in noise—and making it himself; in the sound of the forge hammer, the pile-driver, or the blows of the axe. To the end of his days he was never happier than when beating drums, firing guns, or letting off fireworks.

His education had begun in the traditional manner with being taught to read and to sing and to learn by heart from the psalter and service books. He learnt to write late, in a clumsy and difficult hand, and his spelling always remained wild. Unlike Theodore and Sophia, he did not advance to being taught Polish and Latin, and it is not known exactly when or how he learnt the Latin alphabet. Later on, when he was frequenting "the German suburb," he picked up some Dutch and German, and in after years spoke them with erratic gusto. French and English he never knew. His early lessons included elementary arithmetic, and he acquired some geography from a globe given to his father by Dutch envoys. All this amounts to little in the way of formal lessons, and to less than Theodore and Sophia had. In the main, Peter was educated, not by his tutors, but in wholly unorthodox ways, from doing things for himself, from craftsmen, from boon companions, from foreigners. He was gifted with exceptional physique, keen intelligence, great powers of observation, and a good memory. He was very self-willed, and he was not to be baulked by obstacles. Above all, he had insatiable curiosity for the way in which material objects worked. He had an admirable pair of hands, and he enjoyed to the full using them. He had, in fact, a craftsman's bent, an inventor's, an explorer's. Brought up in a country where science was quite undeveloped, by some strange freak of Providence he was a boy born for the then infant Royal Society.

Deliberately kept aloof from any early initiation into state affairs, Peter indulged to the full his own tastes whenever he could escape from the court ritual. At the age of twelve he took to stone masonry; then to carpentry and joinery; even to some printing. He was becoming adept with an axe and in metal working. Later he used to boast that he was proficient in fourteen trades, including dentistry. When he was fifteen, he chanced on an antiquated English boat, which he was told could sail even against the wind. He became fascinated with sailing and then with boat-building. Thus, in the middle of an almost land-locked country, four hundred miles from the sea which he had never seen, he became enthused with that momentous ardour which was to make him the creator of the Russian navy, and of a new capital on the water opening out on to the sea and all that lay beyond.

At this same time the young giant—for so he was growing to be—was making more and more of his "playing at soldiers." He built an elaborate fort; cannon and firearms were furnished from the royal arsenal; drilling and mock exercises were multiplied. Peter had no use for hawks, horses, and hounds, the pastimes of his father and his brother Theodore. The horde of royal grooms and huntsmen were used as "toy soldiers." So were the young nobles holding court offices in his retinue, among whom figured many of the men who were to be his most trusted servitors in after years.

Peter grew fast. In 1689 his mother found him a wife, Eudoxia Lopukhin. She came of a highly connected landed family, had been brought up in traditional, conservative ways, and had nothing but good looks to commend her to Peter. These were not enough to tie him. He soon became estranged. She bore him a son, Alexis, in 1690, and another son a year later, who died as a baby. Peter did not even attend the funeral.

The year that brought a marriage which meant so little brought a political crisis that meant much. The regent Sophia and her government were overthrown and replaced by the Naryshkins and Peter's other adherents. Sophia governed through two principal ministers, her lover prince Basil Golitsyn, the highest of the high, the outstanding example of the new generation of cultivated grands seigneurs on the western model, and Shaklovity, a man of obscure origin, ruthless activity, and determined skill in handling the turbulent streltsy. For different reasons, both made themselves highly unpopular.

Golitsyn was in charge of foreign affairs, and his new policy of active alliance with the traditional enemy of Muscovy, Poland, aroused much misgiving. In 1686 he scored a success by securing from the Poles the final renunciation of their claims to Kiev; but in return he had to enter into active military alliance against the Turks. Three years earlier John Sobieski, king of Poland, came to the rescue of Vienna besieged by the grand vizier. The tide was turned, and the triple alliance of Poland, Austria, and Venice was thrusting back the Turkish forces in Hungary, in the Polish Ukraine, and in the Adriatic. If Poland were triumphant, would she not then turn and demand from Moscow the return of Kiev? If Turkey gained the day, would she not advance to capture Kiev from Moscow, as she had threatened in 1677–8? This was sound justification for alliance with Poland, and it marked a notable step in the linking up of Muscovy with European politics. But it was followed by two expensive campaigns against the Crimea, which ignominiously failed to achieve anything whatever. When Golitsyn returned to Moscow in the summer of 1689 after his second campaign, it proved impossible to gloze over the failure and the losses incurred. The anger and contempt of Peter and his following were openly displayed, and Peter now publicly challenged the position in the state which Sophia had assumed.

Three years previously she had taken the title of "autocrat," hitherto reserved to Ivan and Peter. She was now suspected, with good reason, of aiming at being crowned. A portrait of her was circulated seated alone in full regalia, with an inscription lauding her above queen Elizabeth, Semiramis of Babylon, and the Byzantine empress Pulcheria. Rumours buzzed as to her intention "to rule by her own will," marry Basil Golitsyn, and dethrone the young tsars. The two camps watched each other nervously with the darkest suspicions during those hot summer days, intriguing and counter-intriguing, Sophia in the Kremlin, Peter in his favourite resort just outside Moscow.

At midnight on August 27, 1689, news was brought to Peter that the streltsy were marching to seize him. Barefoot, in nothing but his nightshirt, he leaped on a horse, ordered clothes to be brought to him in a wood hard by, and made off for the monastery-fortress of Troitskaya forty miles away. Actually the news was false: the streltsy were not on the march. But now the gage was down. Peter gathered his supporters at Troitskaya. The foreign officers with their Russian "soldier regiments" stood by him. The streltsy were divided and hesitant. Force proved to be on the side of Peter. Basil Golitsyn and Shaklovity were handed over. The latter was tortured and hanged on the spot. Golitsyn was exiled to the remotest north. He did not die until 1714, but he was never pardoned. It is tragically ironic that this man, whose ideas were so close to Peter's, had no share whatever in carrying into effect Peter's reforms. Sophia was relegated to a Moscow convent.

It is perhaps strange that Peter did not now (1689) undertake the task of ruling. He was seventeen, full grown and forward, quick in intelligence. He had just had alarming proof, if he needed it, of the importance of politics. In fact, he was but an overgrown boy, and with his own safety assured, he was content to leave affairs in the hands of his mother—a woman, unlike Sophia, "not capable of governing"—and of his supporters, headed by his uncle Leo Naryshkin and prince Boris Golitsyn, a distant cousin but inveterate rival of the exiled Basil. Peter returned with avidity to his hobbies, what he called his "games of Mars and Neptune."

These "games" continued for another five years (1689–94), now combined with more and more frequent contacts with foreigners and "the German suburb." Here, hobnobbing with Dutch and English merchants in a haze of tobacco smoke or indulging in "quadriduan revelling," inspecting some new mechanical device or following the latest news (very belated) of William III's war against Louis XIV, Peter consorted with Anna Mons, the daughter of a German wine merchant, a fair-haired beauty who was for some years his mistress.

Among the foreigners figured the upright Scots soldier of fortune, Patrick Gordon, the most valuable of the foreign officers; but the best known of Peter's early favourites and his especial confidant was Lefort. A vivacious adventurer from Geneva, "able to drink like a hero," he captured and held Peter's intimacy and counsels by his versatile ingenuity and enthusiastic, disinterestedly abandoned attachment. Peter loved him "as Alexander Hefæstion" and, when he died (1699), buried him with almost royal —but Lutheran—honours.

Peter's friendship with foreigners did not mean that he cut himself off from Russians. He surrounded himself with a motley following of nobles and gentry, whom he put through the same paces as himself, giving free and fantastic vein to his lifelong addiction to nicknames. There was, too, a strong sprinkling of men of low or dubious origin, among them Alexander Menshikov, later reputed by his numerous enemies to have started life as a pastrycook's boy selling pies in the streets of Moscow. He rose rapidly in Peter's favour, and after the death of Lefort became for years his closest friend, loaded with the highest honours and responsibilities.

Peter retained throughout his life his youthful zest for crass buffoonery and horseplay, often of the coarsest kind, as well as for riotous drinking debauches. There is no easier charge to make than that of drunkenness, but all foreigners in seventeenth-century Muscovy agree that nowhere else (save perhaps in Sweden) had they come across such prodigious drinking among all classes. Certainly when they entertained themselves they did so with completely uninhibited gusto. Peter's drinking bouts, newfangled in outward aspect, were in line with old Muscovite custom. Disgusting though they are to modern taste, they may well have been less socially harmful, as a late eighteenth-century panegyrist of Peter argued, than the gambling séances of Catherine the Great's time, when estates and serfs were bartered away with reckless prodigality.[8]

Combined with such excesses went elaborate and sumptuous masquerades, as popular in Muscovy as then in Europe. Peter's gross taste debauched them far too often into licentious and blasphemous orgies. To the end of his days, whenever possible, Christmastide, Twelfth Night, and the carnival before Lent were celebrated each year with fantastic rites. The best known of these ghastly enter-

---

[8] The same admirer of Peter, Golikov, also maintained that affairs of state did not suffer from Peter's hard drinking. He certainly had a head like a Madeira cask. To compare small with great, lovers of *Guy Mannering* will recall Mr. Counsellor Pleydell's capacity to turn from "high jinks" to solemn law.

tainments was in the nature of a Bacchic parody of carol singing, in which Peter and his notabilities appeared in sledges costumed as the pope and cardinals (or the patriarch and bishops), and revelled with disgusting ritual meticulously devised by Peter himself. Whether this particularly outrageous sporting was deliberately intended as propaganda against ecclesiastical sway is doubtful. More probably it was simply the most glaring example of the iconoclast's passion for coarse amusement and for inflicting the most ridiculous and odious rôles on reluctant participants. Peter was a cruel man, and he loved to make those around him eat or drink or do what he knew they loathed.

Amusements, and education of sorts in "the German suburb," were combined with continuous extension of his "games of Mars and Neptune." Peter's passion for all kinds of boats was deepened by two journeys that he made to Archangel (1693 and 1694). There he made his first acquaintance with western ships, insisted on going on a long expedition in the White Sea, and saw for himself busy shipyards and the gateway of Russian foreign commerce. He also saw at first hand much of northern Russia in these two journeys. Unlike his predecessors, Peter henceforward travelled incessantly up and down his great country, and the old picture of the tsar pontifically throned on high in "white-stoned" Moscow had no resemblance to the new actuality, dressed in foreign style and always on the move.

Meanwhile his "toy soldiers" were multiplied, organized in two regiments of guards, and exercised in mimic battles that ended, in 1694, with what were tantamount to serious manœuvres. In these the streltsy had to take part, and were discomfited, much to Peter's glee. He himself always maintained that the sham fights were staged "with no idea except that of amusement," and they certainly had much of the element of masquerade. The real reforms in training and equipment that made the army into something new dated from later. Nevertheless, it is impossible not to believe that there was no political calculation in the building up of the two guard regiments, in which the rank and file as well as the officers belonged to the nobility and gentry.

Thereby the young tsar was assured of a bodyguard against internal foes.

Apart from personal tastes and habits that persisted in Peter from this period throughout his life, what was of consequence was that he insisted on himself "going through the ranks" in everything that he did. Peter's constant appearances as able-seaman, as bombardier, as shipwright, as journeyman carpenter were not posturing nor horseplay, though he had a large fund of the latter. He acted—not play-acted—thus, firstly for the simple reason that he liked knowing how to do things with his hands from *a* to *z*, and secondly because he came to believe that by himself rising through the different military and naval ranks that he instituted he could thereby set the example for the kind of service to the state that he imposed on all his subjects, and above all on the upper class—service that had no regard for rank or family lineage, and was to be based on first-hand knowledge, hard work, and sharing of toil. What had begun as a self-willed young man's impetuous delight in doing what he liked and breaking all conventions, developed into a more or less conscious attempt to give visible substance to the conception, new to Russia, of the tsar as first servant of the state.

Now in 1695, at the age of twenty-three, Peter was to experience the difference between "games of Mars" and Mars himself. In that year, with the resumption of war against Turkey, he gave himself over from hobbies to national issues. His own position was altered the year before by the death of his mother, and the year after by that of his half-brother, the joint tsar Ivan. From 1696 he ruled alone and in person. Peter had some tenderness in him, if not much, and he had been deeply attached to his mother, though in her last few years she could restrain him little and her own views came to differ almost entirely from his. After her death his family affection was transferred to his young sister Natalia, bright and open-minded, who later on tried to make the best of those dreadful early years in Peter's marsh "paradise" of St. Petersburg.

With the feeble and passive Ivan no difficulties had arisen, and Peter treated him affectionately, for all the radical differences between them. Ivan was assiduous in performance of the traditional rites of the Muscovite court, which his brother more and more avoided and after his mother's death ceased almost entirely to observe. From 1696, when Peter ruled in person as sole tsar, he was to make something new of tsardom and something new of Muscovy. It has been well said that the watchword of Muscovy was "Guard well the treasure of yesterday," that of Peter "Fear not change; strive that to-morrow be better than to-day."

Chapter 2

Azov and Europe

IN 1695 the war against Turkey was actively renewed. Twenty years earlier Muscovy had entered upon her first war (1676–81) against the Ottoman empire,[1] then in control of the Black Sea lands. The fighting had taken place to the south of Kiev in the Cossack lands on the right bank of the Dnieper, which were so long the prey of the contending rivalry of Poland, Muscovy, and Turkey with her vassal the Crimea. War had been renewed in 1687, in alliance with Poland, when Golitsyn twice attempted the novel strategy of striking direct at the Crimea itself. The distances were too great, and on both occasions he failed signally from lack of provisions in face of the delaying tactics of the Tatars.

Thereafter Moscow stood passive, though there was no peace. Her ally, Poland, and Poland's ally, Austria, both heavily engaged against the Turks, pressed for relieving action. Various Orthodox ecclesiastics in the Balkans, alarmed by Austrian victories, multiplied appeals to the Orthodox tsar to save them from the papistical "Swabians" and (less clamantly) to mitigate the yoke of the Moslem padishah. The Zaporozhian Cossacks were inciting trouble in the Russian Ukraine; the Crimean Tatars were raiding heavily and brazenly insulting. So once again "the Moskals" marched.

Peter struck with his main force, not at the Crimea itself, but at Azov, the strong Turkish fortress cutting off the Don Cossacks from the sea. Nearly sixty years earlier the Don Cossacks themselves had captured it, but then they had no backing from Moscow and had been unable to retain it. Since then it had been greatly strengthened and was strongly held. While a subsidiary attack down the

[1] Apart from an unsuccessful Turkish attack on Astrakhan in 1569.

Dnieper met with striking success, Peter himself failed to capture Azov. "We were very boxed up . . . by multiple command," as he later admitted. Efficient engineers were lacking and there were no warships to prevent the Turks reinforcing by sea.

It is wholly characteristic of Peter that he decided at once on a second campaign against Azov, appointed one of the Russian magnates in sole command, sent urgently to Prussia and Austria to hire engineers, and set about building a fleet of war galleys—previously unknown in Muscovy—at Voronezh. This was far up the Don but had good timber supplies and other advantages. Next year (1696) he again besieged Azov, and this time successfully. A Turkish squadron was prevented from bringing in supplies by sea, and the fortress after a stout defence surrendered. Peter immediately selected a site at Taganrog not far off on the open sea for a naval harbour, and a stream of edicts followed for the compulsory colonization and fortification of the new acquisitions and the construction of Russia's first naval station.

A triumphal entry into Moscow was staged with great show, not in the customary religious setting, but with newfangled pageantry devised around Greek and Roman mythological figures. Lefort, as an admiral, rode in a magnificent gilded equipage. Peter, who had served in both campaigns first as bombardier, then as galley commander, appeared in Lefort's suite, on foot, dressed in German style as a naval officer. Moscow murmured.

Two projects were now uppermost: to press forward the war by building a fleet to challenge the Turks at sea; and to make acquaintance at first hand with the West, the home of shipbuilding and navigation, the reservoir of naval, engineering, and gunnery skill, the possible supplier of loans, and the hoped-for allies in a great combination against the Ottoman empire. Early in 1697 the first batches of Russians were sent abroad to bring up to date their military training and to learn to become sailors. They were soon followed by "the great embassy"; two hundred and fifty strong—chaplains, lackeys, guards, court dwarfs, and all—headed by Lefort, with "min Heer Peter Mikhailov" scheduled incognito to learn shipbuilding. A few months late Sheremetyev, a leading noble and noted general, set off for Italy with a large retinue. The education of Russia in the Petrine style had begun.

This was a new departure in the history of his country. Hitherto, not only had no tsar journeyed abroad, but his subjects, with rare exceptions, had travelled to the West only on official diplomatic missions. It is true that a hundred years earlier tsar Boris Godunov had sent a dozen Muscovites to study in the West, but this was a gesture which led to no results and was not repeated.

Besides the education of himself and his subjects in western shipyards, arsenals, and the like, Peter wanted to concert a grand alliance against the Turks. Already at the beginning of 1697 he had concluded with Austria and Venice an offensive and defensive alliance for three years against the Ottoman empire, the first alliance with Austria in the history of Russia. Before half its course was run, it was in jeopardy, and Peter's hopes of a crusade of Cross against Crescent only showed how ill-informed he was of the tide of European affairs. Despite the treaty of Ryswick in the autumn of that same year (1697), which for the nonce brought peace between Louis XIV, the emperor Leopold and William III, the ambition and power of France and the long-protracted riddle of the Spanish succession concentrated all attention on the West. Prince Eugène's triumph on the Zenta (September 1697) gave Leopold the chance, which he seized with avidity, to open peace negotiations with the sultan and turn all his energies against His Most Christian Majesty.

Nor was there the slightest chance of the Dutch or the English committing themselves against Turkey. Even had France and the Jacobites been less dangerous, commercial interests in the Levant would have prevented any active steps. Peter was reduced to his two other main objects, the recruiting of shipwrights, seamen, engineers, artificers, doctors, and other specialists, and the purchase of naval and military material. In both of these objects he met with much success.

At least seven hundred and fifty men were recruited for

service in Russia. Most of them were Dutchmen, but there were also a good number of Italians, Slavs, and Greeks from the Adriatic lands, skilled in the building and handling of galleys. Some English and Scots came, including Farquharson, a mathematician from Aberdeen, to found the first of Peter's "navigation schools," and John Perry, a naval engineer, to work for some years (amidst wild horses and rampant asparagus) on Peter's plan for a canal to join the Don and Volga, a project talked of by the Turks in the sixteenth century, but not even yet carried out. None were outstanding men, and nearly all were but working craftsmen. Only one, Cruys, a Norwegian sea-captain in the Dutch service, rose to high rank under Peter, ending up as an admiral in the Baltic fleet.

Holland was the first magnet, owing to the numerous Dutch connections of Peter and Lefort. He was diverted from his intention of visiting Vienna first, which would have been his wisest diplomatic course, and went through Riga to East Prussia, where he enjoyed himself greatly with the elector of Brandenburg. At Riga, then in the Swedish empire, there had been squabbles with the local authorities, which were later magnified into a deliberate insult and used as a pretext to justify war against Sweden. Prices were running very high, and the embassy thought they were mulcted. Peter was insistent on keeping up the appearance of being incognito, but at the same time he expected to be treated privately to special favours from the authorities. The governor of Riga confined himself to cold formalities, and his subordinates raised objections to the Russians examining the fortifications of the town.

From East Prussia "the great embassy," compelled to abandon travelling via Copenhagen, went by land across north Germany to Holland, the cynosure of all eyes and loosener of all tongues. The tiny house at Zaandam where Peter lived as a carpenter rapidly became famous and is still preserved as a museum, but he only occupied it for a week. Driven thence by crowds of sightseers, he took refuge in Amsterdam, where he spent much time working in the East India Company yards. As a glaring contrast, he had his first experience of an assemblage of European diplomats, gathered for the negotiating of the peace treaty of Ryswick.

In January 1698, after having spent five months in Holland, he sailed over to the Thames in *The Transport Royal*, the latest model in royal yachts, presented to him by his hero, William III. The two sovereigns had their first meeting in Holland and several more in London, on one occasion with Peter in his shirt-sleeves. William's regard increased, and it was due to him that Peter sat to Kneller for the portrait which now hangs in Hampton Court. Peter leased John Evelyn's residence at Deptford, and saddled him with enormous damages. His servants were "right nasty" about the house, and, it is said, the tsar himself ruined Evelyn's prize holly hedge trundling his wheelbarrow through it. "He spent most of his time in what related to war and shipping, and upon the water," including visits to Chatham and Portsmouth, where "a sham engagement" was put on for his benefit. The House of Commons in session and an honorary doctorate of laws at Oxford interested him far less than Woolwich Arsenal, the Tower, and the Mint.[2]

Early in May 1698, he returned to Holland, whence he made his way to Vienna. Venice, his other ally against the Turks and the most profitable centre for improving his galley fleet, he failed to reach. He was about to start thither from Vienna, when news came that four streltsy regiments were in revolt. He hurried home through Poland, but not without sufficient time *en route* to strike up a mutual friendship with the new king, Augustus II, elector of Saxony, a young man like Peter of boisterous physical strength and great ambition, whom Peter had materially assisted in gaining his crown.

France had been carefully avoided: she was the friend of Turkey, the enemy of his friends, and the supporter of a rival candidate for the throne of Poland. Perhaps almost as important in those days of embattled diplomatic etiquette, a Russian ambassador to Paris ten years before

---

[2] There is no record of his having met the Warden of the Mint, the greatest living Englishman, Isaac Newton.

had been slighted in his reception, and no amends had ever been forthcoming. Despite various subsequent diplomatic interchanges, France remained for twenty years outside Peter's ken and in his bad books.

Look now at Peter as he travels in the West, twenty-six years old, in lusty prime; "a prince of very great stature . . . rather stout than thin, in aspect between proud and grave, and with a lively countenance." He wears his natural hair, brownish-auburn, and a small moustache; walks with a raking, loose-limbed stride; displays with pride his powerful hands rough with the callouses of a working shipwright. "He has great vivacity of mind, and a ready and just repartee. But with all the advantages with which nature has endowed him, it could be wished that his manners were a little less rustic." He does not know what to do with his napkin, and he is awkward and gauche in grand company. As far as possible, he avoids it. By the time he reaches Vienna, "although his native roughness may still be seen in him," his manners are improved, being "rather civil than barbarous."[3] He drinks hard, but in society is restrained.

All note the salty pointedness of speech, the quick grasp, and the insatiable curiosity. He mixes with all sorts and conditions, even including Quakers and Jesuits. Both at home and abroad no prince is less cut off from contact with the multitude, usually the besetting limitation of those who are born on high. One peculiarity is displeasing—and ominous. He has a twitch on the left side of his face, at times distorted into a grimace and restless contortion of the hands and body; then he will roll his piercing, rather protruding eyes, showing nothing but the whites. He is rightly judged "a man of a very hot temper, and soon inflamed, very brutal in his passion"; a strange, exceptional

[3] The manners of that day were very different from ours, but on the standard of his western contemporaries Peter is seen to have improved but slowly. Even fourteen years later (1712) a Prussian courtier can describe how well Peter behaved at a private dinner with the king and queen of Prussia by saying that he never once belched or farted or picked his teeth, "at least as far as I heard or saw."

figure who strikes some as little more than a playboy mechanic. Others, more discerning, marvel that "the providence of God . . . has raised up such a furious man to so absolute authority over so great a part of the world."

This first journey to the West, lasting eighteen months in all, was part turning-point in Peter's career, part confirmation of his ideas and tastes. First and foremost, it entirely confirmed him in his determination that Russians must be sent abroad for education, though it did not alter his conception of that education as primarily technical and utilitarian in the narrow sense of the word. Throughout the rest of his reign a continuous stream of Russians were sent for duty to the West.

Already before departure from Russia, Peter was consumed with interest in all things technical and mechanical, above all in those pertaining to the navy and army. His new experiences immensely enlarged and deepened these interests. Besides his zest for gun-foundries and cartography, mathematics and astronomy, he was indefatigable in visiting and inspecting all sorts of scientific collections and curiosities, from microscopes and barometers to salamanders and swordfish. He picked the brains of all and sundry, from anatomists and botanists to mineralogists, from Dutch merchant burghers to Fellows of the Royal Society.

He was still continually asking, "what is that for? how does that work?", but he began to realize the place of theory and design and, for all his continued delight in manual labour, he came to have an inkling of scientific method. He is reported to have often said that "if he had not come to England he had certainly been a bungler" in the art of shipbuilding: the Dutch could not teach him the theory of design; the English could. Ever after he preferred English master shipwrights to any other, and they became the mainstay for his ships of the line.

"The great embassy" was a turning-point in that for the first time Peter was brought face to face with the complex realities of the European diplomatic stage. He himself, despite his incognito, was in actuality the decisive voice in the groping and clumsy efforts of the Russian diplomats.

They had much to learn, but they learnt quickly. Meanwhile, he returned to Moscow with nothing of his broad diplomatic aim accomplished. Peace, not war with the Sultan, was the *mot d'ordre*. He found to his cost in Vienna that the emperor was already well advanced in parleys with the Turks. In the stead of Turkey there began to arise the idea of a league against Sweden. There was much talk of Sweden between Peter and the elector of Brandenburg. They signed a treaty in which Peter agreed to support Frederick in his coveted aim of the title of king, but common action against Sweden was the subject only of verbal assurances. On his way home through Poland there was more talk of Sweden with Augustus II, who was thirsting for a chance to distinguish himself and to regain Livonia from Sweden. Peter returned to Russia with his mind turned towards new possibilities in the north.

He returned, moreover, with the ineffaceable impression of what wealth, trade, manufactures, and knowledge meant to a country in terms of power and prosperity. He had known at second hand that Muscovy was backward in these respects, but his journey to the West was a turning-point, in that now he had personal, concrete experience of the material superiority of the West. At the same time he had an equally strong conviction that Russians could learn, and learn rapidly, to match the West. He did not explore the springs and motive forces of this western achievement; he did not seek to understand the workings of financial, political, or administrative institutions; and he had little or no conception of the slow and varied stages by which England or Holland had grown to be what they were. What never left his mind was the forest of masts on the watersides of Amsterdam and London, symbols of enriching trade reaching out to the Indies and all parts of the world; the clusters of busy towns, the creation of that independent, middle class, rich in invention, industry, and initiative, which his own country so much lacked.

No contrast could be more violent than the capital to which he hastened back, there to finish off his old enemies the streltsy. Their revolt had been crushed without overmuch difficulty, mainly through superiority in artillery, but

Peter suspected political plotting and his sister Sophia. Already just before leaving for the West a plot against his life had been discovered. The principal ringleader was a streltsy commander, formerly an adherent of Sophia, and among those incriminated were several highly placed personages. Peter immediately struck against them with drastic severity, but did not delay his departure.

Now, in the autumn of 1698, he was determined to unravel what lay behind the revolt of the streltsy, and to deal once and for all with these "begetters of evil." As a contemporary diarist in Moscow records: "It had come to pass that Muscovy was only to be saved by cruelty, not by pity." Wholesale investigations, pushed to the extreme with torture, revealed that talk had been circulating among the streltsy that Peter had died abroad (or in another version was to be done away with); that now was the time to seize Moscow, destroy the foreigners and Peter's lieutenants, and set on the throne his little son Alexis or Sophia. Incriminating letters to the streltsy from Sophia and one of her sisters were alleged.

To Peter all this smelt of the murderous *coup d'état* of 1682. He now revenged himself with a blood-bath of public executions, in which some of his principal counsellors personally took part. Whether he himself also acted as one of the executioners is extremely doubtful, but it was so reported at the time by the Austrian envoy and was widely believed throughout Europe. Thereby Peter's relations with Vienna were still further worsened. In all nearly twelve hundred streltsy were hung or executed, often after fearful mutilation, and their dead bodies were left deliberately displayed to the populace throughout the winter. Droves were sent to Siberia; the remainder were disbanded and expelled from Moscow. Never again was the old capital to be threatened by these turbulent citizen-soldiery, so closely linked with the past and so hostile to Peter's ideas and ways. Henceforth his opponents could count upon no organized, armed force.

Sophia and her sister were forced to take the veil. They never reappeared, and died some years later. About the same time Peter immured his wife Eudoxia in a nunnery, which was the equivalent of divorce. For two years past he had been attempting to induce her to withdraw voluntarily into a nunnery, but she refused to deprive herself of her son Alexis and of the pleasures of the world, and in the end force had to be used. Peter took charge of Alexis.

Moscow was accustomed to torture and savage punishments, but the scale and ferocity of the retribution wreaked upon the streltsy went beyond all memories. Henceforth Peter stood out as a tsar of implacable will and tempestuous violence, in whose hands were bruising irons of wrath. The effect in Europe was for a time to confirm the belief that Muscovy was a barbarous country, and that its ruler, whatever his western tastes, was but an oriental tyrant at bottom. Bishop Burnet, who had been much with Peter during his stay in England, showing him St. Paul's and exchanging views on religion, at first thought that "the Czar . . . will become a great man"; a little later, appalled at the news of the streltsy massacre, he wrote in his *History of His Own Time*: "How long he is to be the scourge of that nation, or of his neighbours, God only knows." In Russia semi-official defence took the line that in a dangerous illness a doctor has to use extreme measures; in a dangerous storm a captain has to jettison cargo.

The blow struck against the old Muscovy as represented by the streltsy was by no means the only such blow that followed Peter's return from Europe. In the following two to three years a number of innovations or reforms were introduced which, though they were not constructed to one plan and bore all the marks of Peter's hasty impetuosity, had the effect of beginning the transformation of the old Muscovy into something new.

On the very day after his return to Moscow took place the well-known scene when with his own hands he shaved off the beards of his principal nobles. Shortly after he proceeded to cut off the long sleeves of their surcoats, and Hungarian or German dress was prescribed for the court and officials. Later, various enactments regularized beards and dress, with the final result that all save peasants and the clergy must shave their beards or pay an annual tax, and even the peasants had to pay a small sum, if bearded, on each entry into a town. All men and women, save peasants and clergy, must wear foreign styles, according to detailed prescription, on pain of fine. Sumptuary laws were nothing new to Muscovy (or to the West), and, as has been already pointed out, both shaving and foreign fashions had been filtering in among the upper class during the previous thirty years. To these upper class what was startlingly novel was Peter's own handiwork, rather than the measures themselves. Among the court, the officials and many of the nobility—especially among the women-folk—they were accepted without overmuch difficulty.

To westerners, the long, flowing robes and high, conical hats of Muscovite costume smacked of the East and aroused the amused disdain with which those who consider themselves superior in civilization nearly always regard the strange habiliments of inferior breeds of humanity. At the court of Versailles a Muscovite mission struck somewhat the same note as a Siamese; they, too, were outlandish barbarians. Peter was determined to be done with this. He himself regarded the Muscovite costume as something not national but of Tatar origin. Certainly his subjects abroad would do better in western dress. This was to be adopted, as one edict ran, "for the glory and comeliness of the state and the military profession." It was more practical and convenient, and it should lead to less lavish display in dress.

If western costume and shaven beards were part of Peter's policy "to sever the people from their former Asiatic customs and instruct them how all Christian peoples in Europe comport themselves," he had little or no success outside the upper ranks of society and the army and navy. The extension of these measures to the merchant-trading class and town-dwellers, and in part even to the peasants, aroused bitter feelings and determined opposition. In all times and in all countries the mass of people are easily touched to the quick by external changes in what they are proud of and habituated to. The beard, with its halo of apostolic sanctity, was not to be parted with by the old-fashioned Orthodox. It was Peter's treasury that gained through the beard tax, not the process of Europeanizing Peter's subjects. During the coming years shaven chins and German dress became bugbears and symbols of oppression throughout the country.

Tobacco and smoking were coupled with foreign costumes and foreign shaving in the denunciations of the old-fashioned devout. Tobacco, long current among foreigners in Muscovy, was officially banned, though for a brief period Peter's father had licensed its use and made it a state monopoly. It was, however, allowed in the Ukraine, and the practice of smoking was creeping into Muscovy. Despite continued ecclesiastical censure, Peter not only followed in his father's hesitant footsteps, but encouraged smoking, partly because he liked it, especially as a means of bringing in money. After several unsuccessful attempts, he contrived to make a monopoly agreement while in England with his eccentric friend the Marquess of Carmarthen. Thereby he gained badly needed ready money, though the English contractors had unending difficulties in Russia and made little profit. Smoking became a habit and the tobacco excise a valuable addition to the revenue.

A far more important addition to the revenue was obtained as a result of a far-reaching reorganization of local government and finance effected in 1699. This provided for the administration of towns (and in the north of country districts as well) by elected burghers, in place of the unpopular and all-powerful sheriffs appointed by the central government. The new law also placed the collection of indirect and certain direct taxes in the hands of merchant-trader bodies and created a new department in Moscow (*Rathaus, Ratusha*), which became in effect a second finance ministry and already by 1701 was handling two-thirds of the revenue. Peter drew the idea of the new municipal bodies from Holland, and he saddled the new institutions with unpopular, and unnecessary, foreign names, but his own share in this piece of legislation, unlike all his other major edicts, was slight. It was the work of Russian merchants and fiscal administrators, and was to a large extent based on projects for taxation reform that had been discussed twenty years earlier.

The same quest for increase of revenue and resources, which inspired so largely the law on municipal reform, was apparent on all sides during this period of anxious preparation for war. Two instances may be given. The initial steps were taken towards starting a new centre for the iron industry in the Urals. Secondly, Peter, with characteristic enthusiasm, put into effect a scheme for a lucrative stamp duty, to be levied on various forms of legal documents. The project had been propounded by Kurbatov, a highly intelligent freed serf, who had journeyed to Italy with his master Sheremetyev. Kurbatov was the first of a new type of resourceful, inventive "profit-makers" (as they were called) whom Peter recruited from the lower classes to devise fresh means for bringing money into the treasury and developing the resources of the country. It is almost needless to add that these "profit-makers" caused "wailing amongst all the populace."

Of all the rapid innovations that followed Peter's return from Europe, far the most engrossing to the tsar himself and the most onerous for the whole country was the creation of a fleet and a new army. The capture of Azov inspired him with the determination to expand the fleet that he had begun to build, and with it to challenge Turkish command of the Black Sea and pave the way to the conquest of the Crimea. Already in the winter of 1696–7, before setting out for the West, a large shipbuilding programme was started on the Don at Voronezh, to be carried out partly by the state and partly by "companies" financed by the large landowners, the church, and the merchants. The programme included ships of the line and frigates, besides galleys and transport vessels. A new ministry, the admiralty, was created, and the embryo of what later became the vast province of Voronezh-Azov began to take shape. Peter was indefatigable in recruiting foreign shipbuilders and seamen. From Sweden he acquired three hundred guns. At Voronezh he spent long periods in charge of construction.

There, far inland, hundreds of miles from the sea, on a shallow, winding river, Italian, Dutch, English, and Russian shipwrights vied with each other in creating Russia's first navy. The burden on the "companies" was very severe; on the rest of the population extra taxation was levied; the demands for labour were voracious; all quarters were combed for carpenters; the Voronezh region was buffeted with exactions. Much of the timber was unseasoned; the foreigners quarrelled with each other; sickness was rampant, desertion rife. Yet, despite all obstacles, the driving force of "the tsar-carpenter" did succeed in fitting out a fleet of sorts. The Dutch minister, a knowledgeable critic, reported on it in highly disparaging terms, but even he admitted that the sixty-gun *Predestination,* designed by Peter himself and constructed solely by Russians, was a fine ship. Already by the summer of 1699, when he went down to Azov, he had the satisfaction of putting to sea with fourteen warships and of despatching his envoy to Constantinople in a forty-six gun frigate, to the disgust and consternation of the Turks.

The immense outlay on the Azov fleet continued even though it was now Peter's ardent hope that his two years' truce with Turkey could rapidly be replaced by a peace which would leave him free to act against Sweden. Nor, when in 1700 that war began, was there much abatement of the corvées and requisitions for the southern fleet and its base at Taganrog. He was already dreaming of a fleet on the Baltic, but, when he had finished with Sweden, he would turn again against Turkey.

He thought in terms of a short struggle in the north. Even so it was a reckless blunder to plunge against Sweden when he had scarcely begun the creation of his new standing army. In later years he acknowledged how blind he had been. His plans were not ready until the end of 1699. In the following nine months a force of 30,000 men was raised, almost entirely infantry, mainly by means of a compulsory levy on landowners. It was as far as possible designed so as to conscribe the amorphous medley of domestic serfs and monastic retainers and thus to spare the working peasantry. They were to be trained and equipped on up-to-date models, worked out in detail by Peter himself. All the commanding officers and many of the junior officers of the new regiments were foreigners.

They gave little satisfaction, and Peter set about recruiting a thousand Moscow gentry as officers. This was the first step towards the compulsory state service for all landowners which came later.

Thus in three years, 1698–1700, Muscovy was thrust forward with unsparing vigour by her young, helter-skelter ruler. Something like the haphazard outline of a new Russia may be discerned: an up-to-date and standing army, a fleet, reorganization of finances and local and central government, development of the iron industry, adoption of western dress and customs, education at home and abroad. In great part the changes were the violent, dramatic acceleration of what had been hesitantly growing during the previous thirty years. In most of what Peter did he had in mind the needs of war, and at this stage of his life he thought almost solely in crude terms of state power; but it is misleading to say that the progenitor of his new Russia was the Great Northern War upon which his country was now to be launched. Banish for a time the knowledge that the struggle that began in 1700 is known to posterity as the Great Northern War; that it dragged on for twenty-one years and resulted in the downfall of Sweden and the emergence of Russia as a European power; that Charles XII proved himself a bizarre military genius of indomitable obstinacy; that the tsar won for himself the titles of "father of his country" and "Peter the Great." Much might have been otherwise. None guessed such an incubus or such an outcome, least of all Peter himself.

Chapter 3

Narva and Poltava

SWEDEN HAD BEEN the enemy of Novgorod and Moscow ever since the thirteenth century. Thereafter she had joined with Poland in defeating Ivan the Terrible's long-sustained bid for the Baltic (1558–81), whereby she established herself in Estonia. Later, when Muscovy was rent with civil war in the so-called Time of Troubles and the Poles held Moscow and installed a Polish tsar, Gustavus Adolphus took his share in armed intervention and deprived Muscovy of her only foothold on the Baltic, the provinces of Ingria and Karelia at the head of the Gulf of Finland. Later he conquered Livonia from Poland, and Sweden rose to be the premier power in the Baltic. In 1700, besides these provinces, she still held western Pomerania (with Stettin, controlling the mouth of the Oder, Stralsund, and the island of Rügen), the port of Wismar in Mecklenburg, and Bremen and Verden lying between the Elbe and the Weser, and giving her a dominating position at the outlets of both these rivers into the North Sea.

Under tsar Alexis the major task of foreign policy had been the reconquest of lands lost to Poland and the future of the Ukraine, but one of his ablest ministers counselled otherwise, urging that access to the Baltic was vital, and that Riga, not Kiev, should be the goal of Muscovite arms. There was a brief war with Sweden (1656–8), in which Alexis, forestalling Peter the Great's campaign nearly half a century later, captured the mouth of the Neva and the Ingrian coast. He failed, however, in an attempt against Riga, and simultaneous setbacks in the Polish theatre of war convinced him that he must not repeat Ivan the Terrible's experience of war against both Sweden and Poland at the same time. A truce with Sweden was followed in 1661 by the peace of Kardis, by which the Muscovites relinquished their gains. Poland remained of primary concern, and Muscovy continued to be cut off from direct communication with the West, save by the circuitous White Sea route, ice-bound for half the year.

The close of the seventeenth century seemed propitious for old scores against Sweden to be wiped out. Denmark, often enough the ally of Muscovy against Sweden, was only too anxious to take the opportunity. Augustus II, the new king of Poland, confident in the reliable army of his hereditary electorate of Saxony, was fired with far-reaching ambitions and hankered after the reconquest of Livonia. The Empire and the western powers appeared to be absorbed in the issue of the Spanish succession. Brandenburg-Prussia, which under the Great Elector had administered the first setbacks to Swedish ascendancy and the renown of the Swedish army, could be counted upon to be neutral and might even be cajoled into participation. Sweden herself was internally divided, her treasury disordered, and her army and navy in poor shape. Her new king was a mere youth of seventeen, whose tight-lipped masterfulness seemed to find chief vent in fantastic athletic feats and spendthrift intrepidity.

So, during the course of 1699 the alliance of Russia, Saxony and Denmark against Sweden took shape under the initial impulsion of Augustus II. He was ardently abetted by Patkul, a refugee noble from Livonia, who had protested violently against Charles XI's policy of "reductions," by which the nobility were deprived of much of their land and privileges. For his pains he was declared guilty of high treason, whereupon he fled abroad and eventually took service with Augustus. He was sent to Moscow, where Peter, who had already made a treaty with Denmark, as had Augustus, welcomed the Saxon proposals for a similar alliance against Sweden. With Brandenburg no agreement was reached. A tardy and abrupt approach by Peter failed, and his appeal to the "moral alliance" concluded verbally between himself and the elector at their meeting in 1697 fell on deaf ears. In the treaty with Poland it was expressly stated that for Russia the object of the war was to be the regaining of the lost provinces of Ingria and Karelia, and that Russia would not declare war until she was assured of peace with Turkey. Peter likewise insisted on this proviso in his treaty with Denmark. At all costs he was determined not to face a two-front war, as had his forbears.

These negotiations were conducted personally by Peter in the utmost secrecy under the very noses of a special Swedish embassy to Moscow. He succeeded in fobbing off the Swedes with protestations of friendship and the solemn reconfirmation of the previous Russo-Swedish treaties, though his duplicity stopped short of renewing his oath to abide by them. Complaint was made of the treatment of himself and "the great embassy" at Riga in 1697, as if they were "enemies or spies," "barbarians and Tatars"; but the matter was not pressed hard. Only next year when war was declared was it given much exaggerated notoriety as a deliberate insult justifying Peter's recourse to hostilities.

Meanwhile, it took twelve precious months to complete peace negotiations in Constantinople. While Austria at the end of 1698 scored the great success of the peace of Karlowitz, Russia only obtained a two years' truce. Although in fact Russian diplomacy was much to blame, Peter considered himself basely abandoned by the Austrians, "taking no more notice of him than a dog." Many years later he was still harping on the desertion at Karlowitz. "I shall never forget what they have done me, I feel it, and am come off with empty pockets." The fiasco of the first Austro-Russian alliance ever concluded had prolonged consequences. Never until the very last year of his reign was there serious rapprochement again with Vienna.

Though left alone to deal with the Turks as best he could, Peter began by pitching his demands extremely high, and in so doing adumbrated a programme of Russian foreign policy for the next century and a half. Not only was he to keep his conquests, Azov, Taganrog, and certain fortresses on the lower Dnieper, which gave him control of the Zaparozhian Cossacks and cut the communications of the Crimean Tatars with the west: Kerch was to be ceded, and thereby access to the Black Sea and a key vantage-point in the Crimea secured. Free navigation of the Black Sea and the Straits was demanded; so, too, the return to the Greeks of the Holy Places in Jerusalem (lately wrested from them by the Latins), and unhindered rights of Russian pilgrimage to Palestine. The sultan was to guarantee to his Orthodox subjects freedom of religion and no excessive taxation. The payment of annual tribute, disguised as "gifts," to the Crimean khan was repudiated. (None had been actually paid since 1683.) Russia was to have permanent diplomatic representation at Constantinople on the same footing as the other powers.

The Turks would listen to little of this. In particular, they were adamant in preserving the Black Sea "as a pure and immaculate virgin." In January 1700, Augustus began the war with Sweden; a few months later Frederick IV of Denmark followed suit. Peter had already modified his instructions: "peace was very, very necessary." But his envoy at Constantinople niggled away dilatorily, and the treaty was not signed until July 14. The Russians relinquished the Dnieper fortresses, and in the end gained only Azov and Taganrog, repudiation of tribute to the Crimea, the right of pilgrimage, and the right to a resident minister on the Golden Horn, this last a major acquisition. On the same day (August 19) that Peter received the news of the signature of the treaty of Constantinople, he declared war on Sweden. On that same day the treaty of Travendal was signed: Denmark had collapsed.

The misjudgments and miscalculations of the three allies were grave enough in themselves, but their crowning mischance was that their young adversary suddenly proved to be a military leader of the rarest stamp. While the Saxons attempted an unsuccessful surprise of Riga and thereafter scored but trifling successes in Livonia, while the Russians waited for peace to be signed with Turkey, while the Danes marched into Holstein, Charles XII decided to strike a lightning blow at his nearest and consequently most dangerous neighbour. Supported by the fleets of his allies, England and Holland, he crossed the Sound and forced the Danes to make peace on the outskirts of Copenhagen (August 19).

Peter could scarcely have gone to war at a more untimely moment. His new army, nearly 40,000 strong, was cumbrously massed against the Swedish stronghold of Narva, a port of consequence at the junction of Estonia and Ingria. Charles transferred his troops across the Baltic to Livonia, and after incredible exertions and gross Russian errors suddenly appeared before Narva, threw the enemy into total confusion in a snowstorm, and ignominiously routed them (November 30, 1700). The odds against him were more than three to one. The Russians lost almost all their artillery and numerous prisoners, including many generals. The old-fashioned cavalry and irregulars took to flight without fighting. The new infantry levies proved "nothing more than undisciplined militia," the foreign officers incompetent and unreliable. Only the two guards and one other foot regiment showed up well.

"This terrible setback," as Peter fully acknowledged it to be, not only exposed Russia most dangerously, but showed that it would be long before a regular army could be trained on up-to-date lines. Would Charles give time for this? His counsellors urged him to concentrate on Russia; to foment discontent; even to proclaim Sophia; if necessary to march to Moscow. Charles, in utter disdain of such contemptible foes, chose otherwise, turned to take revenge upon Augustus, and for six years bogged himself in the sponge of Poland.

Peter, who had not been present himself at the battle of Narva, showed at his strongest in deep adversity, and hurried forward all possible defence measures. Russia displayed all that resilience with which she so often astonishes the world in her darkest moments. Peter set himself three tasks: to raise, equip, and train an efficient standing army; to reconquer Ingria, while holding the Swedes on the defensive in Livonia; to keep Augustus and his Polish supporters somehow in the field. The first and greatest task took fifteen years for full accomplishment, but long before that he had achieved the essentials.

His soldiers were conscripted by levy after levy on the peasants and townsfolk; so many recruits from so many households, usually one from twenty. They were to serve, not as heretofore for the duration of the campaign or the war, but for twenty-five years. The system thus introduced came to stay. It lasted until 1874. From the landowners Peter demanded compulsory service. He still had to rely largely on foreign officers, most of them Germans, but from the end of 1706 the chief commands were given to Russians. In 1702 he issued a proclamation, widely distributed in the West, opening Russia to all foreigners (except Jews), and promising them, besides free passage and employment, full religious toleration and special law courts. This was intended, above all, to attract military men and skilled artisans. The foreigners had a hard task to live down their wretched showing at Narva, and the fact that they received much higher pay than Russians added to their unpopularity.

New training, new discipline, new tactics were evolved, mainly on Austrian, French, and Swedish models, on the basis begun so hastily in 1699. Entirely new training manuals were necessary. Previously only one infantry training manual had ever been published in Russia. It dated from 1647, and was an adapted version of a German manual of 1615. In practice the "troops of foreign formation" had been drilled and trained according to the varying views of their foreign commanders. Their tactics had been based on antiquated versions of the experience of the Thirty Years' War, with musketeers, pikemen, and line formation. Since then western armies had been revolutionised by flintlocks and bayonets and improvements in artillery. Peter had realized the out-of-date inferiority of his army, and had gone to school to the West, but with over-sanguine impetuousness had gambled on quick results. Narva showed how little headway he had made.

He began again, with untiring energy and meticulous personal attention to detail, relying especially on Weyde and aided by certain other foreigners and a small group of Russian commanders. The first thirty to forty thousand flintlocks and bayonets had been bought in England at the time of "the great embassy." Production now began at home; scarcely 6,000 in 1701, but more than 30,000 in 1706; in 1711 annual production was up to 40,000 with a new type of bayonet. The musketry drill and fire control were progressively overhauled. A wholly new innovation was introduced: the bayonet was to be used as an attacking weapon, instead of, as hitherto in the West, in passive defence. The great tradition of cold steel in the Russian army was due to Peter.

In the same spirit, the cavalry was trained "not to fire . . . before the enemy has been put to confusion, but to attack with swords only." The cavalry, which was far the weakest element in the army, made very slow progress: "many times have I spoken about the insufficient training of the dragoons" was Peter's comment when he received the news of the defeat of Mur (1705), due to the cavalry losing their heads. Gradually Menshikov made it into an efficient arm, and a special, new type of light corps was devised, known as the "corvolant," combining cavalry, mounted infantry, and light artillery.

Russian siege guns had always had a good name, but the field artillery was obsolete. After the losses at Narva, Vinnius, a Russian-born Dutchman high in Peter's favour, for a time did wonders in reconstituting the gunnery park. New iron-works and powder-mills, as well as cloth-mills and sail-works, began to swell the home output of munitions and supplies, which was all the more necessary in that imports were now almost confined to Archangel owing to the Swedish blockade in the Baltic. The rise of the new heavy industry in the Urals was specially significant. Between 1701 and 1704 seven iron-works were built there, and the Demidov family began their long industrial reign in the Urals. By 1705 the English envoy in Russia was reporting on the artillery "as at present extremely well served"; and some years later "the iron itself is admirably good, better than that of Sweden, though the cannons [made in the Urals] are said to be indifferently tempered." When Peter had his revenge and captured Narva (1704), Ogilvie in command "never saw any nation go better to work with their cannons and mortars." By 1709 new types of light artillery were in service, and the infantry were being closely supported by three-pounders.

The need for discipline was very strongly emphasized, and in accordance with the customary practice of that day punishments were very severe. In Peter's eyes discipline was necessary in order to fight well: he had no use for elaborate parade-ground manœuvres with troops who "play the fencing master with their muskets, and march as if they were dancing"; nor for the elaborate uniforms of western soldiers looking like "dressed-up dolls." The spirit of his new army was to be infused with devotion, not to "the interests of his Tsarish Majesty," but, as Peter substituted with his own hand, "to the interests of the State."

Slowly, and this time surely, in spite of innumerable difficulties, of constant desertion in the rear, of many delinquents among the landowners, of much quarrelling and jealousy between the generals, Peter forged his new army, organized in divisions and brigades, serviceably uniformed, well equipped and munitioned, gradually tempered in fighting experience. But the burden was immense.

Peter accomplished his second task, the reconquest of Ingria, between 1701 and 1704 by a series of determined amphibious actions on Lake Ladoga and the river Neva against small Swedish detachments manning strongly fortified positions. These successes were followed by the capture of Dorpat (Yuriev)—"this domain of our ancestors" —and by the storm of Narva (1704). Peter now had his revenge. In the meantime, on the Livonian flank the Swedish forces had been given two sharp rebuffs, and devastation and deportations on a terrible scale were carried out. In the Ingrian operations, which Peter conducted in person, Menshikov particularly distinguished himself. From this time forward for many years he was not only Peter's most intimate, and most richly rewarded, friend, but his right-hand man in the war: "mein liebste Kamerad," "mein Bruder," "mein Herz." His energy, initiative, and unvarying optimism, combined with very considerable talents as a commander in the field and with a certain experience of the West, made him invaluable to his master, whose affection and trust even weathered the strain of Menshikov's extortionate rapacity and colossal scandals.

Near the mouth of the Neva, close to a Swedish post that he had captured, Peter founded in 1703 the famous city that bore his name. From the first it was his "para-dise," his "darling," upon which he lavished without stint all his care and without remorse thousands of lives and millions of roubles. Fortification and defence inevitably were uppermost, but within a few months of its foundation he is writing for flowers to be despatched, "especially those with scent"; the peony plants have arrived in very good condition, but no balsam or mint: send them. In later years he would pour out the most detailed instructions for the beautifying of St. Petersburg with trees: 5,000 lime trees from Holland; 500 chestnuts, yews, and replanting with oak or maple; in the end all citizens were to plant the streets with maples. This lay far ahead; in the early years it grew very slowly, with hardly any commerce. Several Swedish counterattacks had to be beaten off. As guardian fortress from the open sea Peter constructed Kronstadt, hard by at the mouth of the Neva.

By 1705 his third task was becoming more and more difficult. Charles must be kept involved in Poland so that he could not invade Russia. Money and Russian contingents had been sent to aid Augustus and his Polish supporters, but he had met with nothing but defeats in the field (1701–4). Yet Charles could not achieve decisive success. Poland officially was not at war with Sweden until 1704, but Charles from the first treated the unhappy country as a mere battlefield. The Poles, though exacerbated with Swedish exactions and depredations, were divided, and in Lithuania the great families of Oginski and Sapieha indulged in a private civil war against each other, paid respectively by Peter and by Charles. In July 1704 Charles went to the length of declaring Augustus dethroned, and causing a rump diet to elect as king an undistinguished Polish nobleman, Stanislas Lesczyński.

This action by a foreigner, and a Swede at that, still further alienated much Polish feeling, but the star of Augustus was low. To give him stronger backing Peter concluded a treaty with his Polish supporters, promising Livonia and more assistance (August 1704). A large Russian army advanced as far as Grodno. The Russian contingents which had been fighting in conjunction with

the Saxons and Polish guerrillas had shown mettle, but
Peter was under no illusions as to what would be the result
of a general engagement of his Grodno army with Charles.
When Charles moved against it, the Russians, despite
much quarrelling among their commanders, succeeded in
hastily withdrawing to Kiev (spring 1706). After some
hesitation, Charles, uncertain of his rear and unprepared
for further attack eastward, decided to force Augustus to
the wall by invading his hereditary Saxon dominions.
Augustus finally collapsed, and by the end of 1706 made
peace and acknowledged Leszczyński as king of Poland
(treaty of Altranstädt). He even handed over Patkul to
Charles, although he was then in Peter's service and
Augustus knew that he would be straightway executed,
which he was.

Now, "this war lay only on us," as Peter put it. He did
his utmost to improve his defence measures, to obtain
new allies, to build up resistance in Poland, and to seek
the means of peace. The War of the Spanish Succession,
the traditional alliance of Sweden with France, and now the
victorious position of Charles in Saxony, at loggerheads
with the emperor, put a premium on high bidding and
counter-bidding between France and the Allies for
Charles's support. Marlborough drove right across Germany from The Hague to Altranstädt, where the two
great commanders met for the first and only time in their
lives. Allied diplomacy was successful in preventing
Charles from intervention against the emperor and diverting him eastwards. Russia was of immediate concern to
the Allies only in relation to their war, and Russian diplomacy was playing from a weak hand. It was further weakened by the death a few months earlier of Golovin, Peter's
able and popular foreign minister (August 1706).

Very early in the war Peter had been open to peace
proposals, and he now sought mediation in all possible
quarters, insisting only that he retain St. Petersburg. Negotiations for an alliance with England (amongst other countries) were entered into but reached no result. Now that
Augustus had capitulated, Peter sought to raise up a rival
against Leszczyński as king of Poland. He offered the

crown to Prince Eugène; a wild idea that was followed by a wilder, that of placing on the throne of Poland Rakóczy, the obdurate leader of the Hungarian rebels against the emperor, who was in league with the French. Peter's long and involved intrigues with Rakóczy brought him no advantage, and served but to confound his relations with the emperor.

From the welter of doubt and confusion there emerged at last one clear decision. In January 1708, Charles XII marched east across the Vistula, at the head of 46,000 men, the best army that he ever commanded. "He believes," said one of his generals, "that he is an agent of God on earth, sent to punish every act of faithlessness." Peter must share the fate of Augustus. "Poland," Charles told Lesczyński, when he pleaded for peace and alleviation of the misery of his subjects, who had suffered even more from the Swedes than the Russians, "Poland will never have quiet as long as she has for a neighbour this unjust tsar, who begins a war without any good cause for it. It will be needful first for me to march thither and depose him also." He went on to talk of restoring the old régime in Russia, cancelling the unpopular reforms and abolishing the new army. "The power of Muscovy, which has risen so high thanks to the introduction of foreign military discipline, must be broken and destroyed."

Peter himself had every reason to know how unpopular he was and how strained was the situation at home. His only son, Alexis, now eighteen years old, showed the utmost distaste for the military and state affairs in which his father tried to train him, and sided with "the long beards," Peter's name for the ultra-conservative clergy, who in their turn cursed Peter and all his works.

In civil affairs all was in strenuous disarray. The central government lumbered along, in all vital matters dependent on Peter's unflagging energy. He was always on the move; never more than three months in one place; now in St. Petersburg, now in Lithuania or Poland; now in Smolensk, in Moscow, in Voronezh; on the Dvina, on the Dnieper; never resting, disporting himself far more rarely than in the past. There was always with him his personal chancellery, headed throughout the reign by Makarov, a man raised by Peter from a minor provincial post in the civil service to be his invaluable cabinet secretary.

The finances were chaotic; labour services and taxes were multiplied, among them an extortionate government salt monopoly. In a desperate attempt to stop tax evasion and embezzlement, Peter instituted in 1708 a new service of revenue officers, called by a foreign title "fiscals," who made the name a byword for extortion, graft, and police spying. "God loves the truth-bearer; the tsar loves the tale-bearer." An attempt was made to remedy administrative confusion by dividing the country into eight gigantic governorships (1708). This reform, though it may have contributed something towards immediate military needs, brought no alleviation in the malpractices and burdens of local administration.

Among the landowners there was constant shirking of service, much disaffection, endless tirades. The peasantry were harried by conscription and forced labour of every kind. The beginnings of St. Petersburg and the Baltic fleet added a host of new burdens. The other western innovations aroused unabated hostility, which hardened into strange and dangerous shapes among the ignorant, superstitious, sprawling masses.

Peter knew well his own unpopularity from the reports of the secret police. It was said: "If he lives long he'll make an end of all of us [serfs]. I am astonished that he hasn't been put out of the way before now. He rides about early and late at night, with a few people and alone. He is the dark enemy of the peasants, and if he races about Moscow much longer, he'll lose his head one of these days." Some said he was a changeling, the son of Lefort, and had fallen in love with the German faith. Others said: the tsar went over the sea to the realm of glass,[1] and there the Germans nailed him up in a cask and threw him into the sea, and a German came back in his stead. Among

[1] Stockholm: the Russian word for glass sounds rather like Stockholm in popular parlance. The expression "German" was used for any western foreigner.

the schismatics he was "the man of sin, the son of perdition, the Anti-Christ"; obey him not; pay no taxes to him; conceal yourselves "in the deserts, as the Prophet Jeremiah ordered the children of God to flee from Babylon. The years of the Lord have passed; the years of Satan have come." Of a truth the seal of Anti-Christ was apparent—the little cross pricked into the left hand of each recruit for the army.

In the words of a later, widely discussed sermon, "our much rebellious Russia is . . . agitated with calamitous storms." In the autumn of 1707 revolt flamed out among the Don Cossacks. Eighteen months before, Astrakhan had rebelled. In the Urals the Bashkirs once more were up in arms (1705–11), "a cursed, numerous and warlike people," killing and plundering all Russians indiscriminately, "for, say they, they are of one faith with the profiteers," the officials and land speculators, who requisitioned the Bashkir horses and land, stiffened the tribute moneys, and searched relentlessly for army deserters. Peter's new mines and foundries in the Urals were in jeopardy, hence also his munitions. These difficult, seminomadic folk were Moslem and linked thereby with the Kazan Tatars: their emissaries filtered through to Turkey; might there be a general Moslem upsurge on the Volga stimulated by the sultan, distant though he was?

In any case, the lower Volga lands were like tinder. For some months in 1705 and 1706 Astrakhan was in the hands of the rebel populace, led by schismatics and other malcontents from up-river towns. Sheremetyev and troops from the western front had to be sent to recapture it.

By good fortune the Astrakhan flame did not spread, but in the autumn of 1707 the steppes took fire. At the very time when Charles XII started for Moscow and was beginning to drive the Russians before him through eastern Poland, the revolt of Bulavin—the most serious of the reign—was in full blaze. Its immediate cause was Peter's attempt to round up by force the runaways and deserters fleeing for refuge to the Don. The revolt was a repetition on a smaller scale of that of Stenka Razin a generation earlier (*cf.* above, p. 16). "And the bandits said among themselves that their business, said they, is with the landowners . . . and the profiteers and the officials, to hang them." As usual in such peasant revolts there was no real political programme, and it was not professedly against the tsar, but against "prince and magnate, profiteer and German," and the introduction of "the Hellenic faith." Bulavin's manifestoes appealed to the Cossack "barebacks," the runaways, the flotsam and jetsam of the frontier, the schismatics, the deportees toiling in hateful Taganrog and Azov, the labourers conscripted for the equally hateful shipyards at Voronezh.

Bulavin himself was a Don Cossack ataman, but the bulk of the older, privileged Cossacks held aloof. There was incitement of the Zaporozhian Cossacks and danger of the Ukraine rising against "the Moskals," but divisions were too deep and organization too lacking. Nor did the revolt spread to the central core of Muscovy. Still, all the Don country and much of the lower Volga was completely out of hand for nearly a year. Troops badly needed elsewhere had to be diverted to smash the rebel bands. So serious was the position at one moment that Peter planned to take the field himself against Bulavin. The repression was merciless: "This rabble," he wrote, "cannot be pacified except by cruelty." By good fortune the worst was over by the summer of 1708 before the full brunt of the Poltava campaign.

During these critical months, beset with the menace of Bulavin in the south and of Charles in the west, Peter was laid low with several attacks of fever and was unusually on edge. One personal matter of great consequence gave alleviation. In November 1707 he was privately married to his mistress Catherine, who was eleven years his junior and had already borne him three children. She belonged to an obscure family in Lithuania, and had been taken into the household of a Lutheran pastor in Livonia, where she fell into the hands of the Russians. Of very little education but of some parts, comely and buxom, she attracted Menshikov's attention, who brought her to the notice of the tsar. Soon she took the place of Anna Mons, but unlike that flaxen, scheming beauty she played her cards well, and proved indeed for the rest of his life to be a wife exactly suited to Peter's needs.

Their correspondence reveals an unfamiliar side of Peter; the affectionate care of a rough man of action for her health and happiness, gifts of watches or Brussels lace, hankering for more letters, family jokes and hopes and fears. Robust and active, but without political ambition, she shared his interests and tastes, was his almost inseparable companion, and came to exercise some restraining influence on his increasingly explosive fits of passion. But the marriage with this foreign servant-girl aroused widespread antagonism, and was a lasting count against Peter among the old noble families.

Early in 1708 Charles began his advance eastward through Poland. At the very outset first Peter, then Charles, were almost captured in surprise sorties at Grodno. The Russians withdrew, carrying out a scorched-earth policy and avoiding any large-scale encounter. Unlike the retreat of Alexander in 1812 in face of Napoleon, the retreat of Peter was from the first conducted according to a general plan of using the great spaces of Poland to waste Charles's forces and of harrying them in minor engagements without running the risk, still considered by Peter too high, of a big, pitched battle. None the less, there were three sharp encounters which cost Charles dear though they did not stay his advance. The British minister, then with Charles in the field, reported that "the Swedes must now own that the Muscovites have learnt their lesson much better than they had either at the battles of Narva or Fraustadt. . . . 'Tis true their cavalry is not able to cope with ours, but their infantry stand their ground obstinately, and 'tis a difficult matter to separate them or bring them in confusion if they be not attacked with the sword."

At first Peter was in doubt whether Charles would make for Novgorod and Pskov and thence for St. Petersburg, or direct for Moscow. Lewenhaupt was in Riga with a strong corps, and this made the former direction more likely. In fact, Charles considered the Livonian region to have been too badly devastated to support a campaign, and his objective was a blow aimed at the centre, Moscow.

By mid-September (1708) he stood on the Russian frontier, sixty miles from Smolensk, in front of which Peter had concentrated his main forces. Then Charles changed plan. The land ahead, though Russian, had been worse scorched than the Polish and the forests rendered virtually impassable. Charles decided to swerve to the south towards the Ukraine, well stocked with provender, and sweep up towards Moscow from the south-west instead of by the direct route from the west. He counted on a valuable ally in Mazepa, hetman of the Ukraine, who at this moment abandoned Peter, but he had not yet been joined by Lewenhaupt, marching from Riga with 11,000 reinforcements and a large, desperately needed baggage-train.

Charles accepted too readily information that proved to be erroneous as to Lewenhaupt's exact whereabouts. He did not wait for him, but turned towards the Ukraine, thereby widening the gap between the two Swedish forces. The Russians interposed, and at the battle of Lesnaya (October 9) heavily defeated Lewenhaupt, who lost almost all his baggage-train and could only join Charles with a shattered fragment of his corps. This "mother of Poltava" greatly heightened the morale of the Russian troops. Peter, who took part in the battle, was justifiably elated, in particular because the victory had been gained over a purely Swedish force.

Further success followed. The news came that up in the north a strong Swedish bid from Finland to capture St. Petersburg, which caused him much alarm, had miscarried with heavy loss. Equal initial alarm was caused by the desertion of "Judas Mazepa," but it soon proved that the Ukrainians would not follow him. The Swedish advance guard was too slow. Menshikov, in rapid and ruthless action, seized Mazepa's artillery and stores, captured and destroyed his little capital, and part terrified, part bribed the Ukraine into submission. Already in November 1708 Peter was writing that "the people of Little Russia stand, with God's help, more firmly than was possible to expect."

Mazepa had not allowed for the Ukraine becoming the main centre of operations. For all the pent-up feelings against the Muscovites, in the bitter winter that now followed the exactions of the Swedes drove the population not to support them, but to wage guerrilla war against them. Behind Charles stood Lesczyński, and dreams of Ukrainian independence from Moscow faded before fears of renewed subjection to Poland and forced acceptance of the Uniate church.

Peter not only succeeded in stifling any substantial Ukrainian help to the Swedes, but by speedy and well-planned operations prevented them from finding a way northwards towards Moscow, or eastwards to Belgorod or Voronezh. Charles was compelled to plunge into the Ukraine, and there to pass a very severe winter. He was unable to draw any help from Lesczyński's supporters in Poland, for Peter was unremitting in aiding his own supporters in Poland with money and troops to prevent reinforcements joining the Swedes in the Ukraine.

Charles likewise failed in his efforts to win the active alliance of the Turks and Crimean Tatars. He succeeded only in gaining over the Zaporozhian Cossacks, unruly irregular cavalry, who in fact contributed no solid assistance and paid for their desertion of Peter by the total destruction by Menshikov of the Sech, their fortified headquarters near the Dnieper cataracts. Yet for a time Peter's position seemed very dangerous. Had the Turks and the Tatars joined Charles, the whole of southern Russia and the Volga lands, still seething after Bulavin's revolt, might have fallen into the enemy's hands. Peter, who himself spent much of the winter at Voronezh re-equipping the fleet, spared nothing to keep the sultan from war. He reinforced the Azov garrison, fitted out his ships, and staged in person a large-scale demonstration to impress the Turks (April–May 1709). In the end the sultan did not move, and ordered Devlet Girei, the bellicose khan of the Crimean Tatars, to give no aid to the Swedes.

In midsummer (1709) the final issue was joined. Charles would neither retreat across the Dnieper nor await reinforcements far away in western Poland. He insisted on

laying siege to the little town of Poltava. The defence wa
stout and, though the position itself was not of great mili
tary consequence, it acted as a magnet for both side
Peter still regarded a pitched battle against the redoubt
able Swede as "a very hazardous affair"; none the less, o
July 8 it took place. Charles, hitherto untouched thoug
in the van of many hundred fights, had just previousl
been severely wounded in the foot, and his generals i
command held divided counsels. Very few of their thirt
pieces of artillery were serviceable; ammunition and pow
der were short.

The Russians had seventy-five guns and excellent pow
der and were greatly superior in numbers, over 40,000 t
22,000, apart from irregulars who took no part in th
actual battle. The numerical odds were not so great a
those at Narva and certain other Swedish victories, bu
the Russian troops were now well seasoned and wel
served, and their morale was as high as that of the Swede
was low. Yet for several hours the Swedes fought desper
ately. Peter himself was in the thick of the battle: he ha
a bullet through his hat, and another through his saddle
while a third is said to have grazed the cross around hi
neck. In the end the Swedes were overpowered and sur
rendered in large numbers, among them most of thei
principal leaders. The remnant withdrew in disarray to th
Dnieper, where, finding their boats burnt, they capitulate
to the pursuing Russian cavalry (July 12). Charles him
self, however, together with Mazepa, succeeded in escap
ing to take refuge in Turkish territory at Bender.

And so "this battle finished with the eternal glory o
His Majesty and the Slavyano-Russian nation." More
modestly he himself described it as "a very outstanding
and unexpected victory:—in a word, the whole army o
Phætons have received their quittance. . . . Now the final
stone has been laid of the foundation of St. Petersburg."

Chapter 4

The Pruth and the Baltic

POLTAVA WAS DECISIVE in that the Russians were now free from invasion, and free to concentrate against the Swedes in Finland, Livonia, and Estonia. Naturally they felt encouraged in great projects of expansion and "in their more than human endeavours to root themselves where once they get footing." Peter's immense labours on his new army had justified themselves to the full. At once Russia's international position was transformed, and her diplomacy spoke with a new, pronounced confidence. A marriage with a foreign princess was now assured for the tsarevich. Within six months the northern alliance was reconstituted, with the addition of Brandenburg, and Peter set about reinstating Augustus upon the throne of Poland. It took longer to conclude a treaty with the elector of Hanover, soon to be king George I, but one year after Poltava Peter gained most of what he wanted, in return promising to guarantee George's acquisition of Bremen and Verden (July 1710). He was now fully embarked amid the complicated currents and cross-currents of north German politics which were for so long to lead Russia so far for so little return.

For some time these treaties did not lead to any combined hostilities against Sweden, except on the part of the Danes. Owing to entanglements with Great Britain and Holland and the vicissitudes of the War of the Spanish Succession, the utmost that Peter's diplomacy could achieve for the time being was the neutralization of the Swedish forces in western Pomerania, but he was at least assured of the upper hand in Poland and free passage through that country.

Meanwhile, immediately after Poltava he initiated two highly successful campaigns from his own frontier. In June 1710, while the Danes unsuccessfully attacked Scania, Peter captured Viborg and cleared the Swedes from

Karelia. In July Sheremetyev reduced Riga, and the conquest of Estonia followed rapidly. An attempt on Viborg made some years earlier from the land side only had failed. Now Peter had enough of a fleet to attack decisively from the sea also. Viborg was an important fortress and centre for Swedish offensive movements. "Now, by God's help," he wrote to Catherine, "it is a strong pillow for St. Petersburg." Two new portents had appeared: Russian ships of the line in the Baltic, though very few as yet, and Russian galleys in quantity, admirably suited to operations among the multitudinous islands lying off the Finnish coast.

Riga had capitulated after a long investment under stress of "the wrath of God" as Peter called it, "that is the plague," from which the Russians suffered quite as severely as the inhabitants. Livonia had been promised by Peter to Augustus and his heirs, but it remained in Russian hands and oaths of fidelity had to be taken to the tsar. On his part the ancient customs and privileges were declared restored, the Lutheran religion was respected, and the Baltic German nobility and Riga merchants were left to dominate the country as earlier. Almost the whole country had been fearfully wasted, but now at least it was left in peace and recovery was fairly rapid.

In the same autumn (1710) the little principality of Courland, lying to the south of Riga, was assured to Peter. He married his niece Anna[1] to the duke, who died a few months later, whereupon a Russian garrison was installed to secure Anna's position. Courland was a vassal fief of the crown of Poland, and the fact that for the rest of the reign it remained a pawn in Peter's hands caused endless difficulties with Augustus II, as also with Frederick William of Prussia who coveted the duchy for himself.

The marriage of Anna broke new ground. In Muscovy no royal princesses had married foreigners for two hundred years; indeed they had rarely married at all, for few

---

[1] She was the daughter of tsar Ivan V, became empress of Russia (1730-40), and is known as Anna Ivanovna, to distinguish her from Peter's own daughter, Anna, known as Petrovna (*b.* 1708, *d.* 1728).

in Muscovy were deemed their equals in rank. Alexis tried to break loose and marry one of his daughters to a Danish prince, but in the end he failed. Now his son started a new tradition, which he and his successors continued with important consequences.

Such were the first-fruits of Poltava, but other fruits by now were ripe. Having conquered Karelia and the Baltic provinces, Peter wrote: "It is now incumbent on us to pray the Lord God for a good peace." Charles XII thought otherwise.

"The king of Sweden has fallen like a heavy weight upon the shoulders of the Sublime Porte." So runs a Turkish document. He escaped to Turkey, bent on using it to recoup his fortunes by an invasion of Russia from the south. Peter's victory had at first much impressed the Turks, but they refused to agree to his urgent demands for the removal of Charles from the sultan's dominions. Charles had energetic supporters in Orlik, *émigré* hetman of the Ukraine in succession to Mazepa who had died, and in Devlet Girei, the khan of the Crimea, a bellicose russophobe, whose influence in Constantinople turned the scale at the critical moment. French diplomacy also aided Charles. Peter had in Tolstoi an ambassador with great experience and ability in handling the Turks, and he had the help of the British and Dutch missions. After involved moves and counter-moves, the struggle for power on the Golden Horn ended in November 1710, with the sultan immuring Tolstoi in the dank recesses of the Tower of the Seven Bastions and declaring war on Peter.

Whatever his ultimate designs against the Ottoman empire, Peter had no desire at this moment to plunge into war in the south when so much remained to be done in the north. He did what he could to seek accommodation with the sultan before he was committed to fighting, but meanwhile issued orders for an exceptionally heavy levy and hurried on preparations for a bold campaign conceived on lines never entertained by any of his predecessors. His plan, over-sanguine and grandiose as so much else in his undertakings, was to strike in force for the Danube, sweep into armed alliance the two Rumanian principalities of Moldavia and Wallachia, vassals of the sultan, and summon the Christians in the Balkan peninsula to rise against their Moslem masters.

Thus Peter was the first of the Russian tsars to don the mantle of liberator of the Balkan Christians. This rôle, however, was not part of a calculated offensive against the continuance of the Ottoman empire, still less an end in itself. The proclamation that he issued in 1711 as he marched southwards was a hastily contrived means of gaining support from any available quarter in an unwelcome war that had been forced upon him. His summons, which was couched in terms of common Orthodoxy, not of common Slav brotherhood, was specially intended for the Serbs and Montenegrins, to fire them to join the Russians in fighting "for faith and fatherland, for your honour and glory, for the freedom and liberty of yourself and your descendants"; thus would "the descendants of the heathen Mahomet be driven out into their old fatherland, the Arabian sands and steppes."

During his minority, Serbian and other Orthodox Balkan ecclesiastics, in particular alarm at the successes of the Austrians, had appealed to Moscow for succour, and subsequently Peter himself had some relations with these and with a few fighting leaders of those Serbs who had recently taken refuge from the Turks in southern Hungary under Austrian protection and were finding this Catholic tutelage little to their taste. Peter also set special store on recruiting Illyrians from the Adriatic coast for service in his navy and as political agents. Among such was an able, energetic merchant-adventurer, Savva Raguzinsky; that is from Ragusa, a seaport town in Dalmatia. He had been in Russian employ for a dozen years, and in 1711 was Peter's main adviser and agent in Balkan affairs. It is characteristic that Peter should cut loose from the earlier Greek ecclesiastical informants whom he had inherited, and turn to Slavs of the type of Savva or to Balkan guerrilla leaders.

Raguzinsky was now entrusted with the task of raising revolt in the Balkans. His plans must have been very hastily concocted and there was little enough organization, but in the summer his bellows raised the flames in the western Balkans, notably in Montenegro. The Black Mountain fastness, which was ruled by the militant prince-bishop Daniel, had not previously had direct connections with the Orthodox tsar, but Daniel responded eagerly to Peter's emissaries, and in company with his two brothers took the lead in spreading rebellion. It could, however, only be of secondary consequence, for it did not touch Bulgaria, the land between Constantinople and the Danube, or divert the Turks from their operations against the Russian army.

The decisive field was the Principalities. Peter marched south in person, accompanied throughout the campaign by Catherine. He was delayed *en route* by fever, but he despatched a strong advance guard to clinch alliance with the hospodars of Moldavia and Wallachia, and forestall a Turkish crossing of the Danube. Neither task was achieved. Only in April 1711, when Peter himself arrived in Moldavia, did he gain the unconcealed support of the hospodar Cantemir. Two treaties were signed with him. The first provided for military aid and an autonomous status for Moldavia under Russian suzerainty. The second proved the more important: it ensured to Cantemir a safe refuge in Russia in case of necessity.

Cantemir could supply little organized aid. He was at daggers drawn with Brancovan, the hospodar of the much richer Wallachia, who had a sizable army and supplies, desperately needed by the Russians. Peter was unable to win Wallachia over. Brancovan, though he had been in close relations with Peter for some years, would not commit himself irrevocably, and in the end, knowing that the Turks were already across the Danube in strength, thought best to save himself and his country by truckling to their demands.

Meanwhile, Peter pressed forward far down the river Pruth, and detached the bulk of his cavalry to raid the Turkish rear and burn their magazines on the Danube. He was now disastrously short of provisions, and was badly informed as to the Turkish strength and movements. The grand vizier at the head of vastly superior forces succeeded in surrounding the Russians in a battle at Stani-

-leshte near the Pruth (July 19–21, 1711). With his ammunition and supplies exhausted, Peter was forced to seek terms. He avowed that never had he been "in such desperation." This "deadly banquet" cost him dear, though not so dear as he feared. He was prepared in the last resort to accept any terms "except slavery"; to yield not only Azov and his other southern acquisitions, but all his conquests from Sweden, and in addition Pskov and more, all save St. Petersburg.

The actual terms he had to sign were far less severe, though humiliating enough. He lost Azov, his fleet, all that he had gained from Turkey in 1700. He was not to intervene in Poland. Charles XII was to have free passage to Sweden. Thus Peter's southern projects were utterly ruined.

The grand vizier and others were richly gifted according to custom, but it is probable that the tales of Catherine giving up her jewels and of rumbling carts loaded with Russian gold for the grand vizier were later exaggerations to prove treachery when a few months later his enemies encompassed his downfall. The janissaries had had tough fighting and had suffered severely; the Russian cavalry had been successful in destroying the Turkish depôts far to the rear; the bellicose extremism of the Crimean khan was not to the taste of the grand vizier, and he was above all anxious to conclude terms before Charles XII rode into his camp breathing fire and slaughter. He had in fact, achieved decisive gains for his master, though not for Charles or Devlet Girei. Now Turkey would be free to turn against Venice and reconquer the Morea.

If the reasons for the comparative moderation of the Pruth terms are doubtful, the reasons for Peter's catastrophe are clear. He was rash and impetuous, relying on information that was both defective and over-optimistic. The Turks moved far more rapidly and in much greater strength than he allowed for. Above all, he miscalculated the effective aid he might receive from the hospodars and the Balkan Christians. The majority feared to fling in their lot unreservedly with Peter until he had first proved by a victory over the Turks that they would be on the winning side. But Peter was not in sufficient force to achieve such a victory without substantial help from the Christians. "It is dangerous," said one of the Wallachian nobles, "to declare for Russia until the tsar's army crosses the Danube. Who knows, moreover, whether Wallachia in the power of the Russians will be happier than under the domination of the Turks?" After the battle on the Pruth, another of Brancovan's adherents praised his wisdom "in awaiting the decision of a battle in which it has finally been seen that beneath German clothes the Muscovites are still Muscovites." Here in two nutshells is summed up much of the reason for Peter's failure.

The defeat on the Pruth settled the fate of the Montenegrin-Serb rising. Although some initial successes were won, Peter could do nothing but leave in the lurch prince Daniel and the others who had rallied to his appeal. After a tough resistance, the rising was crushed and Daniel had to flee from Montenegro for a time. He made his way to Russia, the first of a long succession of such visitors from Cettinje, and Peter gave him subsidies and portraits of himself, but the Montenegrins and the Serbs were left to face the Turks as best they could. Prince Eugène, not Peter, was about to succeed in the rôle of liberator, when in the war of 1716–18 against the Turks he won for Austria, by the treaty of Passarowitz, a commanding position in the Balkans for twenty years. None the less, Peter was far from forgotten in the Balkans, despite his catastrophe on the Pruth. He had initiated relations with Montenegro which were to continue close for the next two hundred years, and he had multiplied connections with the Serbs which were to bear fruit in the middle decades of the eighteenth century in large migrations of Serbian colonists to the Dnieper steppes.

The terms of the Pruth required to be ratified and carried out. To this end the Turks took hostages from Peter, including his principal diplomat, Shafirov, who had negotiated the peace terms with great skill. Shafirov, a converted Jew by origin, who had made himself indispensable in the foreign office by his excellent knowledge of western languages and his ready ability, was one of those capable, low-born finds of Peter whom he raised from nothing to great influence. For the next dozen years he was one of his most important counsellors. He had his work cut out in Constantinople, where he was twice consigned with Tolstoi to the rats in the Tower of the Seven Bastions; for Peter, once he had marched his army back home, refused to cede Azov and Taganrog until Charles XII had decamped from Turkey. Although Peter soon yielded on this, his action gave additional handle to the war party who were pressing the sultan to denounce the Pruth terms and resume hostilities.

For nearly two years Peter was faced with this dangerous combination of Charles XII, the Crimean khan, Orlik and Lesczyński in conjunction with the "northerners" among the Turks. Twice the sultan was won over to a resumption of war, but on each occasion Shafirov, backed by the British and Dutch envoys, was able to tide matters over before fighting began. Peter set the greatest store on somehow getting Charles removed from Turkey, but he was himself largely immersed in Baltic operations and the main brunt of the struggle necessarily lay with Shafirov in Constantinople. In the end Charles and his supporters overplayed their hands. The Crimean khan was deposed, Charles himself quarrelled violently with the Turks, and in June 1713 Peter was assured of peace by the treaty of Adrianople, which renewed substantially the Pruth terms. Thereby the sultan was free to concentrate on war against Venice and Peter on war in the north.

Peter had not been able to improve on the terms that he had been forced to accept when surrounded in his 1711 campaign. Among those terms was the cessation of permanent diplomatic representation on the Bosphorus. It was a major object to recover this right, but he was not able to do so until 1720, after the great Austrian successes against the Turks had inclined the sultan to seek a makeweight to Austrian influence in the shape of Russia.

The best that Peter could say of the Pruth disaster was that he had got off with fifty blows when he was condemned to a hundred. Not only did he lose Azov and any return for the immense labours on his fleet; not only did his army suffer heavily from sickness; the possibility of peace with Sweden receded still further, while at the same time his capacity to carry on the war was hindered by the Turkish demands for the evacuation of Russian troops from Poland. To a great extent he managed to evade fulfilling these demands, but his position in Poland remained difficult and was rendered the worse by the mounting indignation caused by Russian high-handedness and depredations. War and diplomacy still occupied his main attention, and for the next seven years (1711 to 1717) he was absent from Russia for far longer spells than ever before.

From the Pruth he hurried to Poland and Germany. There he arranged the wedding of his son Alexis to Princess Charlotte of Wolfenbüttel, whose sister had recently married the emperor Charles VI. The marriage was a dreary failure from the start, but it formed a precedent that was followed for the next two hundred years. For the previous two centuries all the Russian royal princes had married Russians. After 1711 they all married foreign, usually German, princesses.

Peter did not return to Russia till January 1712. It was at this moment that his marriage with Catherine was publicly solemnized in St. Petersburg. It was much more than a reward for her sharing the toils of the Pruth campaign. Thereby she became officially his consort and her children received an assured position: as yet there were only daughters; two boys had died as babies. After six months he was away again for nearly a year, mainly with his army in north Germany. He was only back a month before he was off with his fleet on the Finnish campaign throughout the summer of 1713. He was likewise engaged throughout the following summer; 1715 was spent mostly at home, though with much summer cruising at sea. Then in February 1716 he left again for the west, to make his last attempt at an allied invasion of Sweden from Denmark and to pay his first and only visit to Paris. He did not return to St. Petersburg until the last day of October 1717.

During the intervening years St. Petersburg became the

capital, though it was never officially proclaimed such. The fact that Peter, when not abroad, spent so much of his time there or thereabouts inevitably made it the centre of government. The building both of the town and of the fleet and Kronstadt, with frequent changes of plans and with appalling demands of labour, was a ceaseless preoccupation for Peter. Edict after edict was issued drafting carpenters, stonemasons, labourers and yet more labourers from all over the empire; Tatars, Chuvash, Cossacks; so many from Siberia, so many from Kazan, so many from each province. Wages were not paid; desertion was chronic; sickness festered; death battened, in that fir-birch-stunted delta-marsh, with the Neva constantly in flood or arctic winter in grip, where the "tsar-reformer" willed it that his "paradise" should rise.

In the meantime Peter strove to manipulate his allies for the expulsion of Sweden from her territories across the Baltic and for her compulsion to peace. His allies he likened to "too many gods; what we want, they don't allow; what they advise, cannot be put into practice." Each desired to gain something from Sweden—and from each other. They were united only in their alarm at the appearance, for the first time in history, of Russian troops in these north German lands. The close of the War of the Spanish Succession in 1713 added still further complications by setting the participants free for stronger action in Baltic affairs, in particular Great Britain and Holland. Both of them were deeply involved in Baltic and Russian commerce, dependent on Baltic naval stores, and much disturbed by the advent, also for the first time in history, of a Russian navy in these waters.

Military operations were first concentrated on Swedish Pomerania. Stralsund was ineffectually besieged by a combined force of Russians, Danes, and Saxons (1711). Next year Menshikov arrived with larger Russian forces, and sat down, together with Peter, before Stettin. But he had no siege train, and the Danes failed to produce the requisite artillery, despite Peter's heated remonstrances. The Danes also failed to prevent large Swedish reinforcements being shipped across the Baltic, though they caught their empty transports. Stembok, their commander, struck across from Pomerania to Holstein. He moved too quickly for Peter, and beat a Danish force in Mecklenberg, but Peter pursued him into Holstein, defeated him (January 1713), and left Menshikov and the Danes to finish him off. This was not accomplished till May. Affairs in Holstein were even more complicated than usual by the fact that the duke was a boy of twelve, and that chief, though not sole, influence lay in the hands of Goertz, a chameleon of a diplomatist, shortly to be the exceedingly ingenious and unpopular factotum of Charles XII.

During these years (1711–13) Peter's health began to give serious concern. In 1711 for the first time he went for a cure to take the waters at Carlsbad, where he was very restive and complained to his absent wife of feeling cooped up in prison under the wooded hills. He always hankered after big spaces and long views, though within doors he liked small, low rooms (without black-beetles, which he could not abide), and he had a strong distaste for large palaces. Later, Pyrmont in central Germany was substituted for Carlsbad; then Spa; and in his closing years some newly discovered waters at Olonets, not very far from St. Petersburg, but almost inaccessible except in winter by sledge. He stoutly maintained that these Russian waters, though in fact of very dubious worth, were far superior to any abroad, but at least he could be kept contented there at the neighbouring iron-works. As would be expected, he was the despair of his doctors (two of whom were Scotsmen) and had not the slightest compunction in playing ducks and drakes with their prescriptions, especially where cucumbers, salted lemons, or Limburger cheese were concerned.

Peter was travelling abroad now with all the prestige of a great and powerful monarch, in very different guise from the first journeying to Europe of the unknown young ruler of an unknown country. But though his main preoccupations, both now and in his later travels, were political, he always retained his passion for curiosities, mechanical contrivances, scientific exhibits, and suchlike. Still he delighted to pick the brains of all and sundry and secure recruits for the advancement of Russia.

Among the last figured the famous philosopher and polymath Leibniz, who had long followed with close interest the career of Peter and the rise of Russia as a possible bridge between Europe and Asia. They met for the first time in 1711, and several other times later on. Leibniz never came to Russia, but Peter paid him a salary as adviser on educational, legal, and administrative reforms, "in some sort the Solon of Russia." For a number of years the great savant plied the tsar with memoranda, notably on an academy of sciences, reform of justice and government and various geographical and scientific projects. Leibniz was one of those who contributed to the westernizing of Russian institutions, which became so marked a novelty in the last years of the reign. More and more, in fits and starts, Peter was turning his mind to a radical reorganization of administration and government, and he was imbibing in his western travels new conceptions of the functions of the state and the duties of the citizen.

For the next three winters after his return to Russia from Holstein in the spring of 1713 internal measures and the cleansing of the Augean stables of the administration absorbed much of his capacious energy, but he continued to be mainly preoccupied with efforts to force Sweden to conclude peace. Prolonged attempts at negotiations through a conference at Brunswick, summoned by the emperor Charles, were wasted labour: it was "much like a dovecote—one ambassador flies in, while another flies out," and the contestants could not be brought together.

Confident that his Baltic fleet was far enough advanced, Peter decided to strike against Finland, near at home where he would not be encumbered with wrangling allies. He had no intention of retaining it, but it would come in as a useful makeweight in negotiations, and he regarded it as an important source of supplies for Sweden. "If God lets us go as far as Åbo next summer," he wrote, "the Swedish neck will become easier to bend." By the end of that summer (1713) Åbo was duly his, together with

Helsingfors and all southern Finland. The Swedish commander was nerveless and incompetent, and though his successor, a Svencoman,[2] proved his worth in two hard-fought battles, the conquest of the whole of Finland was completed in 1714.

The success of these two campaigns was largely due to the Baltic fleet, which carried out numerous amphibious operations and assured the transport of men and supplies. The major credit goes to the large galley fleet, admirably devised for operations among the legion islands that stud the Finnish coast and make navigation by sail dangerous or impossible. The galleys were adapted from the earlier Azov galleys, and owed much to Italian and Greek seamen from the Adriatic. They were built of fir wood and largely manned by soldiers, of both of which there was an ample stock at hand. It took far longer both to build and especially to equip and man an efficient fleet of men-of-war. As on land before Poltava, Peter issued strict instructions that the ships of the line and the frigates were not to be risked in battle against the Swedes save under overwhelmingly favourable conditions. In 1714 he had the satisfaction of winning in person off Hangö the first Russian naval victory, but it was almost entirely a battle of galleys. Peter returned home in triumph with the Swedish admiral a prisoner, and henceforth August 7 was one of his anniversary days.

The exploits of the Baltic fleet spurred Peter on to increase his building programme, and the construction of a new port was put in hand near Reval. In 1715 the cost of the fleet was more than twice that of 1711. Hardwood timber supplies remained most difficult, for the ship timber from the northern forests was only fir, and the oak had to come hundreds of miles from the middle Volga. Forestry edicts, before Peter's reign unknown in Russia, were multiplied to control timber cutting in the interests of the navy. As the British admiralty in North America, so the

---

[2] The Swedes settled in Finland were styled Svencomans. They had a monopoly of education and administration. The majority of the population was Finnish.

Russian admiralty encountered the maximum of difficulty in enforcement.

To better communication with St. Petersburg a canal was made joining two tributaries of the Volga and the Neva, and another to avoid the tempestuous passage through Lake Ladoga. This latter became a major scandal. It engulfed thousands of labourers (including 20,000 Cossacks from the Ukraine) and millions of roubles, and in the end the army was set to work on it, much to its disgust. After several changes of plan and a series of violent quarrels, it was only completed after Peter's death. The building of the Ladoga canal and the new ports added much to the bitter resentment already seething against St. Petersburg and the fleet; yet Peter inflexibly persisted in his determination to make Russia a sea power.

The men-of-war were in part purchased in England and Holland, but in greater part were Russian built, under the direction of a small group of English master-builders. These were key-men, whose salaries were large and punctually paid, and who were specially favoured by the tsar; "they eat in private with him, they sit at his table in the greatest assemblies." They were thought to be of such consequence that, when in 1719 George I was planning action to stay Peter in the Baltic, the British government tried to entice them home: their return would be "of the utmost consequence to . . . the security and welfare of His Majesty's dominions."

Apart from communication difficulties, Russia was admirably supplied with all types of naval stores of good quality. The earlier ships of the line that were built were very unsatisfactory, but later there was a great improvement. English witnesses, among them high naval officers, bear witness that some at least were equal to the best that England could build, "and more handsomely furnished." The besetting weakness lay in the ignorance and lack of seamanship of the crews. The flag officers and many of the others were foreigners, notably Danes and Dutchmen, a few of whom were excellent and dashing seamen, but the Russian gentry hated the imposition of naval service.

Peter, despite his commanding position in Finland and

Estonia, never dared to risk a full-scale invasion of Sweden across the sea, unsupported as he was by the Danish fleet. Nor could he attempt to establish any blockade of the Swedish ports. The most that could be done was raiding of the enemy coast, and nothing very serious of this kind took place until the closing years of the war. The Swedish neck, so far from bending, proved even stiffer. Late in 1714, at long last Charles XII returned from Turkey to his own country and galvanized it to yet further sacrifices.

By then Stettin had been lost (1713), and nothing remained to Sweden across the Baltic save Stralsund and Wismar. Stettin fell to the Russians under Menshikov, thanks to the belated assistance of Saxon artillery, but Menshikov had only been able to secure its capitulation after involved negotiations, as a result of which Frederick William of Prussia obtained his heart's desire, occupation of the city without striking a blow. Peter upbraided Menshikov for bungling diplomacy: he was quite prepared for Prussia to acquire Stettin, but only after having committed her to fighting against Sweden. None the less, in July 1714 he drew nearer to Frederick William, and signed another treaty with him which he hoped might lure Prussia into active operations.

Hanover, another claimant for the spoils of war without fighting, appeared on the scene with proposals (April 1714) agreeing with the Russian aim of the expulsion of Sweden from Germany, provided that Bremen and Verden went to Hanover. But the Holstein dispute remained unresolved, and in consequence Denmark—always of major importance to Peter since she alone had a fleet and was actively engaged against Sweden—hung back from Peter's reconstitution of the northern alliance. At this juncture the position of Hanover became all the more important, for in August Queen Anne died and the elector succeeded to the British throne as George I. By February 1715 Peter succeeded in persuading the Danes to hand over to Hanover Bremen and Verden, of which they were in occupation, and shortly afterwards the contemptuous recklessness of Charles XII clinched the issue of the northern alliance and actual hostilities.

Charles, adding injury to insults, attacked a Prussian detachment. Thereby even the Prussians were moved from their covetous caution. In the course of the summer (1715) Prussian, Hanoverian, and Danish forces joined in besieging Stralsund. After a stout defence, it capitulated just before Christmas. To Peter's disgust no Russian troops had joined the allies in Pomerania. Augustus was meeting with such serious resistance to his rule in Poland that he persuaded Gregory Dolgoruky, the Russian minister, and Sheremetyev, in command of a Russian army in Poland, that Poland was of more consequence than Pomerania. Consequently the Russians stayed to support Augustus. Peter, who never forgot that troops at the decisive point are the essential, held Pomerania to be at that moment of more consequence than Poland. "I am astonished at Prince Gregory that in his old age he should become a fool and has allowed himself to be led by the nose or . . . As to the tricks of Flemming [Augustus' principal minister] I am not astonished, for such is their plough and sickle."

Peter took the field again in person, and once more moved large numbers of troops and galleys westward, in an effort to impose the lead on his allies and bring Sweden to her knees by a combined invasion from Denmark. His first port of call was Danzig, which he overawed to pay heavily for her continued unabashed trading with the Swedes. There he proceeded to take a step of extremely doubtful advantage. He married his favourite niece, the vivacious Catherine, daughter of Ivan V, to Karl Leopold, duke of Mecklenburg (April 1716), and promised him a Russian garrison, together with Wismar, as Catherine's dowry. Russian troops promptly occupied Mecklenburg, where they remained for nearly three years.

Peter was warned by his diplomats that the marriage would create the worst impression among his allies, especially the Hanoverians, but he had grown to have unbounded confidence in his own capacities and often to treat his ministers as ignoramuses. He was his own master and no one had sufficient authority or influence to oppose effectively anything that he wanted. What precise objects he had in mind in making this marriage remain still unknown. Contemporaries abroad had no doubt: he meant to install himself permanently in north Germany; not content with two gates into Germany, Riga and Poland, he must needs have a third, the Mecklenburg ports, Rostock and Wismar.

Karl Leopold, an aping, tyrannical boor, who even on his wedding-day could not remember to put his cuffs on, so grossly outraged all classes of his subjects that the emperor Charles was called upon to suspend (and later depose) him. Many of the Mecklenburgers had been compelled to take to flight, and had entered Hanoverian and Danish service, among them Bernstorff, George's chief minister. They now spared nothing in abuse of Peter and intrigue against him. The hostility of George as elector of Hanover was combined with the growing alarm of George as king of England at the Russian overthrowal of the balance of power in the Baltic. His British ministers, for all their protests against Swedish interference with British commerce, were far too anxious about their supply of naval stores from the indispensable Baltic to wish for anything but a speedy peace. "We cannot see the ruin and overthrow of a nation in the preservation of which the interests of our people are so deeply concerned." Had it not been for Charles XII's privateers and his intrigues with the Jacobites, British policy in these years might have steered a much more positively anti-Russian course.

The Mecklenburg question, which was to drag on intolerably for more than thirty years, alarmed Denmark little less than Hanover, and she likewise had the liveliest suspicions of designs attributed to Peter in Holstein, including that for a Kiel canal which would avoid the Sound dues. The young duke of Holstein was being befriended by Peter, and next year he was taken by him to Paris. Wismar, in Mecklenburg, the last Swedish stronghold across the Baltic, after a siege by the allies surrendered in April 1716, but the Russian contingent, arriving at the last moment, was not allowed to enter the town. Peter had promised it to the duke, but the Danes hoped to keep it for themselves.

Prussia alone was not seriously alienated by the Mecklenburg marriage. Intense jealousy of Hanover mitigated her suspicions of Russia, and the personal relations of Frederick William with Peter, judiciously oiled by the gift of batches of tall grenadiers for the Potsdam parade ground, helped to maintain his belief that Peter was his least unsure ally for the retention of Swedish Pomerania. But the Prussians did not intend to do any fighting for him.

Such was the most discouraging background of the project for a joint invasion of Scania from Denmark together with a Russian descent from Finland to be covered by the Danish fleet. Peter, notwithstanding his anger at the Danish behaviour at Wismar and the delay of a three weeks' cure at Pyrmont, did his utmost to overcome all obstacles. By July 1716 he was in Copenhagen, had assembled there a part of his forces, and set about reconnoitring the enemy coast.

He depended on the Danes for artillery and for shipping to transport the remainder of the army from Rostock. Delays and difficulties now became intensified and the first harvest of the Mecklenburg marriage was reaped. The transports were not forthcoming, and the Danes would not risk their fleet to cover the contemporaneous Russian attack that was planned from Finland. The British and Dutch fleets, which were in the Sound, could not be won over to join in decisive action against the Swedes. Wrangles over money and supplies were unending. The Swedes, actively engaged though they were on the Norwegian front, had time to reinforce their positions in Scania. Peter's own generals held back from the undertaking, and in September Peter himself came to the conclusion that invasion was too risky and must be abandoned.

He complained to his wife that his allies were like young horses harnessed to a carriage in which the side horses did nothing to help the centre one, but only brought the carriage to a standstill by their wild curvetting. His nominal Hanoverian allies excelled themselves in accusations that he had deliberately abandoned the campaign in order to hold Denmark and the north German coast in custody. In fact, there is little evidence from the Russian side that Peter at this stage had any clear, far-reaching designs in north Germany; his moves and countermoves seem to have been, above all, actuated by his immediate aim of settling with Sweden, either in conjunction with Frederick of Denmark and George I, or independently. His troops promptly left Denmark, and soon after most of them marched off from Mecklenburg. He did not at first abandon all ideas of another invasion plan for 1717 in conjunction with the Danish and British fleets, but by the beginning of that year he was more and more inclined towards a radical change of policy.

By this time Charles XII's most trusted counsellor was the Holsteiner Goertz, who excelled himself both in ingenious manipulation of an almost empty treasury and in the weaving of diplomatic spiders' webs. Subterranean approaches were made by him to the tsar, who already had been receiving hints of mediation from France. He listened, and embarked on a new course which was soon to lead to alliance with France and eventually to peace negotiations with Sweden in the Åland islands. Travelling slowly from Denmark, reinsuring himself with Prussia on the way, laid low in Holland with another bout of illness, in May 1717 he reached Paris.

There Peter stayed six weeks, in a rout of visits, inspections, and dinners. He saw all the notabilities, and was specially attracted by the observatory, the botanic gardens, and the manufactory of Gobelin tapestries (which he imitated in Russia). He directed particular attention to the Academy of Sciences, of which he was elected an extraordinary member. At the Sorbonne he was given an official reception, and was presented with a Gallican plan for the reunion of the Eastern and Western churches. At Versailles he escaped to indulge himself in his usual fashion. But the main object of his visit was high policy, and he brought with him a cluster of his ablest diplomats.

The original proposals for alliance with France lacked nothing in boldness. "Put me," he declared, "instead of and in the place of Sweden. The European system has changed. . . . France has lost her allies in Germany.

Sweden, half annihilated, can no longer be of any succour to you; the power of the Emperor has greatly increased, and I, the tsar, am come to offer myself in the place of Sweden." He would bring Prussia with him, which was essential; also Poland. The Netherlands could be squared. Great Britain was too divided in herself to be a trustworthy ally of France, her late enemy. Such proposals, though not unattractive to the regent, the duke of Orleans, were anathema to Dubois, who had the real control of French foreign policy. The king, Louis XV, great-grandson of Louis XIV, was a mere child of seven, "only an inch or two taller than our Luke" (Peter's favourite dwarf). Dubois was determined to do nothing to prejudice the alliance with Great Britain and the Netherlands, which he had just contrived out of the strange aftermath of the War of the Spanish Succession. The visit of the tsar to Paris was much to his distaste, and he intended to keep him playing and conclude no treaty. But it was also the policy of Dubois to ensure that France, not the Empire, should take the leading part in any mediation for peace with Sweden.

In the end Peter was at least successful in extracting a treaty, signed in Amsterdam in August 1717. France would undertake mediation and, when her treaty with Sweden expired in the following April, would not conclude any new engagement contrary to the interests of Russia and Prussia. The latter power, already on close terms with France, was a signatory of the treaty. Thereby Peter reckoned that French subsidies to Charles XII would shortly cease, and that French influence at Stockholm would work for some settlement with Russia. In fact, French support of Russia was felt first in a very different quarter, at Constantinople; that was very timely assistance, but it did not shorten the Great Northern War. The alliance with France fell so far short of what Peter had hoped that it has been accounted by some as tantamount to a severe diplomatic defeat. But he was quite the equal of his rivals in the number of strings he had ready for his bow, and the treaty of Amsterdam had not been signed before he had concluded in strictest secrecy an agreement with

Goertz to begin direct peace negotiations. A new phase in the Great Northern War was opened, though the meeting of Russian and Swedish negotiators face to face was for various reasons delayed, much to Peter's chagrin, until May 1718. Before then a great storm that had been brewing burst.

Chapter 5

Alexis and the Problem of the Succession

IN JANUARY 1718, after seven years' absence from the old capital, Peter returned to Moscow, at grips with the most baffling problem of his reign. The issue was for him simple, but its resolution most difficult. Would the whole conception of the new Russia he was trying to forge be abandoned on his death by his successor? As yet Peter was only forty-six, but he never spared himself, and he never counted on Providence to guard him from the risks to which he habitually exposed himself. His successor was Alexis, his son by his first wife, Eudoxia Lopukhin. He was by now twenty-eight and had showed clearly enough that he was and would remain the very opposite of his father. "I have let business slide and am an idler," he wrote to the empress Catherine on one occasion. This was in substance true. Worse still, he did not hide his aversion to all his father's predilections. Worst of all, in October 1716 he fled the country and took refuge in the emperor's dominions. Lured back to Russia by Peter's emissaries, he reached Moscow in February 1718. The crisis of his wretched life was reached, and for Peter the crisis of the succession issue.

Alexis for his first eight years had been brought up by his mother Eudoxia and saw very little of his father. Whether it was his mother who instilled in him from the first an aversion to his father is not known. It is probable, but there is no definite evidence. When Peter broke with Eudoxia in 1698, he took Alexis away from her and provided for his education. He was taught Latin, French, and German, and grew up to be a young man of some cultivation, interested in books and western novelties, but mainly as curiosities. He was lazy physically and intellectually, had no capacity for sustained activity and no inclination to turn his bookish knowledge to any practical effect. If he could, he would have liked to sit peacefully at home and enjoy himself. In many traits he took after his uncle tsar Theodore and especially his grandfather tsar Alexis; his father he resembled not at all.

When he was fourteen, Peter took him on his campaign against Narva (1704) and, after his triumphal entry into the captured city, is said to have addressed his young son with a boding homily. "I have taken you on the campaign, that you might see that I do not fear either toil or danger. I am a mortal man and I may die to-day or to-morrow; therefore you must be assured that you will receive little joy if you do not follow my example. You ought . . . to cherish everything that contributes to the welfare and honour of the fatherland, trusted counsellors and servants, whether foreigners or Russians, and you ought to spare no labours for the general welfare. . . . If, as I hope, you follow my paternal counsel and take as the rule of life the fear of God, justice, and virtue, God's blessing will always be upon you. But if the wind dissipates my counsels, I shall not recognize you as my son, and I shall pray God that He punish you in this life and in the life to come."

In the course of the next ten years, Peter devolved various tasks upon the incompetent and unwilling Alexis, but he showed no aptitude either for military or civil affairs. He relied solely on others and, as his father upbraided him, would do or learn nothing for himself, "like a young bird holding up its mouth to be fed." He grew both to loathe and to be in terror of Peter and all his ways, and it seems that on occasion he went to the length of malingering. What his father in fact was demanding of him was a change of nature and character. With a man of Peter's dominating brutality, it was a relationship of tormentor and tormented.

After Poltava, Peter sent him to Germany for a time and, as has been already mentioned, in 1711 married him to princess Charlotte of Brunswick-Wolfenbüttel. The marriage brought no change in Alexis. He saw little of his wife, and soon disgusted her by his drunken ways; a little later even more so by his undisguised preference for a Finnish serf-girl, Euphrosinia, with whom he became infatuated. To Peter this mattered little, but it mattered greatly that Alexis was increasingly identified with "the long beards"—the opposition clergy—and was in occasional communication with his mother in her convent.

In the winter of 1715–16 the future of Alexis seemed about to be decided, but Peter, probably because he was seriously ill, fumbled and for once showed irresolution. Early in November 1715, Charlotte died just after having given birth to a son, named Peter. Within three weeks the empress Catherine bore a son, also named Peter. Peter demanded of Alexis that he either resign his claim to the throne or retire into a monastery. Alexis wrote submissively in reply that he would resign and recognize Peter Petrovich, only a few days old, as heir. Peter did not trust him, and after six weeks' delay sent a second letter, this time virtually requiring him to become a monk if he would not reform his ways and make himself a fit successor to the throne; he could not continue as he was, "neither fish, flesh nor fowl." Without a day's delay Alexis replied that he would enter a monastery. Peter was on the point of leaving for north Germany. He now for the first and only time during these exchanges saw Alexis in person and told him to wait six months before giving a final answer (February 5, 1716). Combining at one and the same time peremptory intimidation with confused vacillation, the father inspired the son with a mixture of abject fear and dissembling desperation.

Seven months elapsed, but Peter had no word from Alexis. Early in September 1716, he therefore wrote requiring him either to join him in Copenhagen for the invasion of Sweden or to go into a monastery. Alexis set out ostensibly for Copenhagen, but he was actually determined on flight to his brother-in-law, the emperor Charles VI. He reached Vienna in November, in company with Euphrosinia, his inseparable mistress. In an hysterical interview with the friendly and reassuring imperial vice-chancellor, he declared: "My father says I am no use for war or governing, but still I have sufficient sense to rule. God is master and disposes of the succession." He appealed frantically to the emperor "to protect my life and assure

my succession and that of my children." He was given
secret asylum in a castle in the Tyrol, whence after five
months he was moved to another near Naples.

The flight of Alexis was a blow both to the pride and to
the interests of Peter which it was imperative to counter.
After long search, he succeeded in discovering the Tyrol
sanctuary. Flight was bad enough; flight to Austria was
worse still, for Peter's relations with Austria, always cold,
were at this time unusually strained owing to the dispute
over Mecklenburg and to Austrian victories over the
Turks. Peter demanded of the emperor the return of his
renegade son. Charles, much perplexed, took refuge first
in silence, then in an equivocal reply, to which Peter retaliated with a second demand couched in strong terms
that aroused lively apprehension in Vienna of some drastic
action by the Russians.

Meanwhile, Peter had despatched Tolstoi, who had
been promoted after his Constantinople mission to his
master's special confidence, to seek Alexis out and secure
his return to Russia at all costs. Tolstoi was armed with
an autograph letter from the father to the son, promising
forgiveness if he returned. Faced with the fertile and re-
lentless Tolstoi, Alexis, after ten days of cajoling, bullying,
and intriguing, was at length persuaded, despite great misgiving, to rely upon his father's promise of pardon and
return to Russia (October 1717). He made indeed two
conditions, which Tolstoi on his own responsibility accepted, with the subsequent approval of Peter: he wanted
to be allowed to keep Euphrosinia (who was with child),
and to live with her on any of his estates he chose. The
emperor Charles, informed of Peter's offer of pardon, was
only too anxious that Alexis should agree to return of his
own accord, though he was not prepared to compel him.
His underlings, however, gave a different impression to
Alexis, who appears to have been brought to the conclusion that the choice lay between willing return in company
with Euphrosinia and desertion by his protectors and
deprival of his mistress.

The last stage was reached in February 1718 when

Alexis arrived back in Moscow. Three days later Alexis publicly acknowledged his guilt in taking to flight and asking the emperor for protection. In a solemn ceremony a manifesto was read depriving him of the succession and declaring Peter Petrovich heir to the throne. At the same time Peter announced that he would pardon him, if he revealed the whole truth in regard to his past conduct. Thus, the pardon was now made conditional. At Naples no condition had been mentioned.

Peter had settled the succession on his baby son, but he had not rid himself of the incubus of Alexis, a political problem of haunting anxiety. Immediately he began a prolonged inquisition, accompanied as usual by torture, into the designs of Alexis and his associates, a variegated and worthless set. Peter himself took the leading part in the investigations. The net widened to include his first wife Eudoxia, his last surviving half-sister Mary, Dositheus, bishop of Rostov, and certain of the highest aristocracy. From February to July, Moscow and St. Petersburg lived in a state of extreme tension. Arrests were multiplied; fear was on every side, that of the government included; for there was little doubt that the sympathies at least of the church and of the common people were whole-heartedly with Alexis.

Alexis himself was subjected to seven interrogations, in which he had to make written answers to written questions. At the end he was twice tortured. His earlier replies aroused Peter's furious suspicions by their confused vagueness: his final testimony, written three days after he had received twenty-five strokes, was an abject self-condemnation. Euphrosinia rewarded him for his obsessed devotion by fatally incriminating statements, for which Peter rewarded her with an ill-deserved pardon and a motley assortment of her lover's belongings.

The suspects were only very rarely confronted with each other, and there were no witnesses in defence. It was not a trial, but a political indictment. The only documentary evidence against Alexis consisted of two letters he had written while in Naples, a copy he had with him of a report from Pleyer, the Austrian minister in Russia, and some notes of Alexis, dating four years back, on Baronius's *Ecclesiastical Annals*.

The two letters from Naples were written to the senate and the bishop of Rostov, though never delivered to them. They contained nothing but generalities explaining his flight and exhorting them to disbelieve rumours of his death and to keep him in remembrance. A third letter written to the archbishop of Kiev was not found. From Alexis' confused recollection it appears to have mentioned hopefully a rising in Kiev. Pleyer's report was far more serious: it told of a plot among the Russian troops in Mecklenburg to kill Peter and put Alexis on the throne. This was one of the counts most heavily pressed against Alexis, but there was nothing to show that he had any connections with the plot, although eventually the confession was extracted from him that he would have joined the rebels if they had invited him.

A further accusation pushed to the utmost was that Alexis had asked the emperor not merely for protection but for restoration, if necessary by force, when Peter died. Only at the very end, after torture, did Alexis make such a confession. It is not definitely disproved by the documents in the Vienna archives.

The notes from Baronius provide what is almost a touch of comic relief in this grim inquisition. Peter read them through and marked two with a cross: Charlemagne's edict on dress, and the killing of Chilperic for depriving the church of its property. Alexis was questioned as to them, but even after torture the Romanov had nothing of interest that he could remember about the Merovingian.

From the welter of heterogeneous recollections, stretching back over many years, from the exculpatory confessions, often made after torture, Peter obtained a picture of widespread loathing of his methods and rule, which was to him all the more alarming in that there was no specific conspiracy to root out but an amorphous opposition to combat, with all hopes centred on a complete change when the tsarevich should succeed his father. Alexis would live peacefully in Moscow; St. Petersburg and the fleet would be abandoned; he would cut down the army; "he did not want to have wars with anyone and wished to content himself with the old dominion." The rights of the church would be respected. There would be an end to the ceaseless levies and the grinding corvées: the landowners would no longer be ruined, no longer be subjected to compulsory service, no longer dishonoured by having to take orders from Menshikov and other upstarts.

Alexis was not the leader of any movement, still less of any planned rebellion. He had no capacities or inclination for such rôles. But as the heir to the throne and with his known hatred of his father, he was the inevitable symbol round which clustered the hopes of all those, high and low, rich and poor, who suffered from the many-sided tyranny of Peter and the crushing burdens of his wars and his new capital.

Alexis had a rash tongue, especially when drunk, and was most incautious in allowing his boon companions to say even more against his father than he himself. He wanted to succeed as tsar, and his acceptance of resignation or a monastery was nothing but terrified submission in fear of his life, a temporary subterfuge which later on could be disavowed on the score of compulsion. As one of his cronies is said to have remarked: "Putting on a cowl doesn't drive a nail into one's head; one can take it off." Peter surmised as much.

Alexis hoped for his father's death, but he had no idea of assassination. "He prefers a rosary to a pistol in his hands," said his German mother-in-law with truth. He drifted, waiting nervously and passively for something to turn up. When he made off for Austria, it was in desperate fear of what Peter might do to him. He believed that he was popular far and wide in Russia: "and of the simple people I heard from many that they loved me." He also believed that many members of the great families were friendly disposed. One of the Dolgoruky princes was, indeed, incriminated and heavily punished by Peter, though he did not strike against the other aristocrats whose names were mentioned as well-wishers of Alexis.

His connections with his mother seem to have been

slight and intermittent, but Peter, ever suspicious of Eudoxia, ferreted out particulars of her most unseemly goings on and condemned a lover of hers to public torture and death. Charging her with political incitement against him, he despatched her to a remote nunnery under strict supervision. Similar punishment was meted out to his half-sister Mary, likewise judged to have encouraged opposition. Dositheus, bishop of Rostov, was accused of connivance with Eudoxia and Alexis, deprived of his orders and broken on the wheel. In all nine persons suffered death publicly in Moscow; nine others were sentenced to hard labour, many others less severely punished.

There remained Alexis. Peter decided that, at the least, he must receive official condemnation in the most public manner. He was declared guilty of attempting to conceal the truth, of plotting against the tsar, and of fleeing abroad to conspire for foreign aid. A special gathering of high ecclesiastics was asked to give opinion as to what punishment was due: they inclined to mercy. The same question was put to a gathering of the senate, the ministers, and the military and civil notabilities of the land. They signed a recommendation of the death penalty, unanimously, one hundred and twenty-seven in all.

Two days later (July 7, 1718), without Peter having confirmed this recommendation, Alexis died in the fortress of St. Peter and Paul in St. Petersburg, having suffered torture twice in the previous week. Officially death was the result of apoplexy. Most contemporaries believed that he had been made away with. It is uncertain precisely how he died, but there is no doubt of the general truth that he had been hounded to death by his father.

Far away among the northern peasants a tale was current right down to the middle of the last century. Alexis was set to build a ship. Peter ordered him to square a beam. He split it badly. Peter in fury hit him between the shoulders with a handspike. Three days later Alexis died. There is the pith of the relationship between that awful, bestriding father and his weak, shiftless son.

Twelve years later another heir to another throne, displeasing son to a regimenting father, attempted to flee abroad from the paternal parade-ground. He failed to escape. His father exploded with threats of execution, but was prevailed upon to substitute imprisonment. The son lived to inherit the throne and be known to the world as Frederick the Great.

Alexis was dead and Peter Petrovich had been proclaimed successor to the throne in his stead. He was the apple of his parents' eyes, as their letters show. From time to time he appeared at celebrations on a diminutive Iceland pony, but he was backward and ailing. Less than a year later, when only three and a half, he followed Alexis to the grave (May 1719). Catherine had now borne four sons and six daughters; all save three of the daughters had died as infants. Later she bore Peter another son, but again to no purpose; he died at once (1723).

The two elder daughters,[1] Anna and Elizabeth, born in 1708 and 1709, were accomplished and attractive children, but they were girls. No woman had as yet sat on the throne, though twice Muscovy had been ruled by female regents, the second time by Peter's enemy Sophia. From his half-brother Ivan V there were only daughters living, Anna, duchess of Courland and Catherine, duchess of Mecklenburg. Thus, there was only one male Romanov who might follow Peter, his infant grandson, Peter, son of Alexis. He had been taken charge of by his grandfather when his father fled to Austria, and he appeared to be healthy, but he was only three years old in 1718, so that if he succeeded Peter there might well be need of a regency with all the additional hazards which that would involve.[2]

Such were the problems of succession that weighed on Peter during his closing years. He seems to have made no attempt to lay down an order of succession, a fundamental

[1] The third living daughter, Natalia, was born in 1718 and died in 1725.

[2] He did, in fact, reign as emperor Peter II, 1727-30. By strange chance, whereas in Russia no woman had ever previously reigned, following Peter the Great's death in 1725 four empresses reigned almost continuously for the next seventy years. None reigned thereafter.

law such as was proclaimed for the first time in 1797 by the emperor Paul and regulated the succession until the collapse of the Romanov dynasty in 1917. Peter had a far harder issue to settle than Paul, but, if he had anticipated Paul, Russia might perhaps have been spared the long series of disputes over the throne that followed his death.

He did, indeed, issue a so-called law of succession in 1722, but it merely declared that the sovereign should be whomsoever he himself named as his successor. It was buttressed by the example of Ivan the Great, but Peter did not, in fact, follow his example, for he did not proceed to name any successor, although in May 1724 Catherine was crowned empress, which was taken by many as indicating that she was to follow her husband on the throne, if she outlived him.

Less than a year later (February 1725) Peter lay dying. He scrawled on a piece of paper: "I leave all . . ."; but his fingers were too weak and he could not finish. He asked for his daughter Anna to be brought into his room. By the time she arrived, he could not speak, and he died, like Charles XII, without having definitely made known any decision on the most baffling problem of his reign.

Chapter 6

The End of the Great Northern War

DURING THE FIRST six months of 1718 the fate of Alexis overshadowed all other issues, even that of the struggle with Sweden. Peter, however, was not so engrossed that he had not time for the new diplomatic course that he had embarked upon in the previous summer, and in May 1718 he was at long last able to start direct negotiations with Sweden.

The conference took place in one of the Åland islands. To it Peter sent Bruce, a Russianized Scotsman who had proved himself in the Finnish theatre of war as one of Peter's best military and naval organizers, and Osterman, an able and patient Westphalian who had entered the Russian foreign office some ten years earlier and had earned Peter's confidence by his incorruptibility and diplomatic skill. In these last years of the reign he was the soundest and most trusted of Russian diplomats, and he was to remain a power for the next twenty years through many vicissitudes. The Åland conference dragged on with numerous interruptions and halts for nearly eighteen months, but though it failed to bring any result it revealed the new international setting, partly of Peter's contrivance, partly of his adversaries', that marked the ending of the Great Northern War.

Peter was by now more and more antagonistic to George I of Hanover and Great Britain, and to Augustus II of Poland and Saxony. He proposed to enter into "confidential friendship and very close engagements" with Charles and broached the far-reaching idea of a new "balance in Europe" based on alliance with Sweden and Prussia, with the guarantee of France. Russia would restore Finland to Sweden, except Viborg, but would keep all her other conquests. Prussia was to keep Stettin and the mouth of the Oder. Goertz, the chief Swedish plenipotentiary, had persuaded Charles XII to let him attempt a settlement with Russia, Sweden's strongest adversary, at the expense of her weaker adversaries in north Germany, where Sweden might regain her lost territories. Thus Peter's line of approach was calculated to fit in with Goertz's intrepid schemes for ministering to his master's pride and salvaging his fortunes.

Goertz had to put up a strenuous fight for the retention by Sweden of various of the Russian conquests, especially Reval, which was considered by both sides to give command of the Gulf of Finland, and he tried to deflect Prussia by promises of Polish territory in place of Stettin. Yet the difficulty of finding an "equivalent" for Sweden might not be insuperable, since the Russians were prepared to abandon Augustus and recognize Stanislas Leszczyński as king of Poland, to leave the Danes to the tender mercies of the Swedes and, above all, to give Charles military and naval assistance in gaining acquisitions at the expense of Hanover, over and above Bremen and Verden.

Some progress was made in discussions along these lines with Goertz, who was seeking at the same time even more elaborate combinations with Alberoni, his Italian counterpart, the chief minister of Spain. It was Alberoni's object to deprive the Empire of the territories in Italy gained from Spain as a result of the War of the Spanish Succession. Against Spain and in defence of the Utrecht settlement, the Quadruple Alliance was formed (January 1718) by the Empire, Great Britain, the Netherlands, and France. Alberoni hoped to disrupt at least one of the allies, Great Britain, with the help of the Jacobites, and he sought the alliance of both Sweden and Russia for an invasion of Scotland.

Nothing was too fantastic for Charles XII, and Peter had no objection in principle to any project which might weaken George I. The Jacobites had already been busy making plans with the Swedes and weaving connections with the Russians. During Peter's visit to Paris the previous year he was in touch with certain Jacobite leaders, and there were Jacobite agents and sympathizers in Russia, notably his doctor, Erskine, and one of his admirals, Thomas Gordon. Neither at this time nor later did he commit himself with the Old Pretender or regard the Jacobites as anything more than pawns in his diplomacy; but inevitably his relations with the Jacobites caused bitter reactions in London.

Peter received the proposals of Alberoni (June 1718) noncommittally. The defeat of Spain in the war in the Mediterranean, which followed in that same summer, and the collapse of the Jacobite attempt on Great Britain next spring (1719) destroyed any hope there might ever have been of effective combination of Spain with Russia and Sweden. Peter was not under any illusions, and instructed Osterman at the Åland conference to agree to support the Pretender only if the Swedes were insistent on this. The success of the Quadruple Alliance against Spain fortified the position of Dubois, who was now in name as well as in fact French foreign minister, and postponed any chance of France veering into support of Peter's idea of a new "balance in Europe." Without that support and in face of new Swedish requirements it proved impossible to come to agreement with Charles XII for an offensive and defensive alliance and joint operations in northern Germany. Nor could Frederick William of Prussia be enticed into any dangerous action against either George I or the emperor Charles VI, much though he desired the discomfiture of their schemes in Mecklenburg and Poland. By November 1718 Peter decided that he must abandon for the time being his wider plans, and content himself with what had always been his primary object, namely, a peace securing his gains from Sweden.

At this same time Osterman wrote to his master that Charles XII "through his foolhardy actions some time or other will either be killed or break his neck riding at a gallop." He proved a true prophet. On December 11 Charles, while besieging a castle in Norway, was shot through the head and died immediately. So ended "Swedish Charles . . . a frame of adamant, a soul of fire":

" 'Think nothing gain'd,' he cries, 'till nought remain,
On Moscow's walls till Gothic standards fly. . . .'
His fall was destin'd to a barren strand,

A petty fortress, and a dubious hand;
He left the name, at which the world grew pale,
To point a moral and adorn a tale."[1]

The death of Charles, although it relieved Peter of so stiff-necked a fighter, brought him for the time being no nearer a successful peace. On the contrary, the chances of a settlement receded. The crown passed not to the duke of Holstein, Charles's nephew befriended by Peter, but to his sister, Ulrica Eleonora, who resigned it a year later in favour of her husband, Frederick of Hesse-Cassel. Goertz and his Holstein faction were swept away, and he himself fell a victim to popular fury and was beheaded. Swedish policy changed from seeking agreement with Russia at the price of concessions in the Baltic provinces to seeking agreement with her other foes at the expense of Russia.

Peter was unable to counteract this swing of Swedish policy against him, either by offering certain minor concessions in his terms or by launching a sharp raid on the Swedish coast near Stockholm. The Åland conference, though it continued in nominal being until October 1719, was in effect dead. In the six months following July 1719, Sweden concluded peace treaties with Hanover, Prussia, and Poland, and an armistice with Denmark. Peter, who throughout so much of the war had suffered from having too many nominal allies, now had not a single supporter. Yet he still remained in a strong position, for he had possession of all that he wanted from Sweden. Nothing but force could deprive him of these gains, and he was powerful on land and at sea. Even though his earlier schemes for peace had entirely failed to bear fruit, his continued resolution in the face of the coalition that was now forming against him in the end rewarded him richly.

Behind Sweden stood George I. He alone might supply the force in the Baltic required to regain something from

[1] Samuel Johnson, *The Vanity of Human Wishes.* It was until recently believed by many that the shot was fired on purpose by one of his own men. It is now generally accepted that this was not so.

Peter. He was busily attempting to cement a coalition of Hanover, Great Britain, the Empire, Saxony, and Poland against Russia and Prussia. In Mecklenburg Hanoverian and Imperial interests sufficiently coincided, at least as against Prussia and the retention of the Russian garrison there. Early in 1719 Peter did indeed withdraw his last remaining troops, but the absentee duke, his nephew-in-law, remained a card in his hands which was to cause much trouble in the future. In Poland Augustus II had fallen out with Peter and was striving to establish a strong, hereditary monarchy and a standing army, and to regain the vassal principality of Courland, still nominally ruled by Peter's niece, the widowed duchess Anna, but actually controlled by the Russians. Both the Emperor and George I backed Augustus in his ambitious schemes and hoped to cajole the Poles by the lure of acquisitions from Russia, even perhaps Smolensk and Kiev.

The central issue lay in the Baltic, where it was British, not Hanoverian, policy that had the final say, since Britain provided money and ships. The object of British policy was peace, but a peace that should preserve enough for Sweden so "that the Tsar should not grow too powerful in the Baltic." With this end in view armed mediation was undertaken and an alliance concluded (February 1720) promising Sweden a subsidy and the continued aid of the British navy to prevent Russian predominance and bring about a favourable peace.

A strong British squadron had already entered the Baltic in 1719, with secret orders if possible to combine with the Swedes and destroy the Russian fleet, but nothing was effected. Peter was not to be intimidated, and refused to accept letters delivered by the admiral in command requesting him to cease hostilities; "letters," as Peter described them, "according to their custom of barbarian haughtiness with threats." In the two following summers a British fleet likewise attempted to force Peter to yield, and on each occasion failed. His galley fleet carried out two severe raids on the Swedish mainland, while he also won a naval action against the Swedes, in which he captured three frigates.

This state of armed hostility between Russia and Great Britain, falling just short of actual war, was accompanied by a break in formal, diplomatic relations, but not in commercial relations. Peter was careful to insist (though by very unskilful means) that his quarrel was with the elector George, not with Great Britain, and he refrained from definite action against British trade. British opinion was divided as to the wisdom of strong action against Russia; the expense of the Baltic fleet was bad enough and the cost of proceeding to the length of war was judged prohibitive. The government was still further weakened by the commotions caused by the South Sea Bubble. The consequent indecisiveness of British aid to Sweden caused disillusionment in Stockholm and readiness to listen to French overtures for mediation. The exhaustion of the country was past bearing: an end there must be. The breakdown of the Åland conference had not prevented Peter from maintaining intermittent touch with the Swedish court. Arrangements were made for another peace conference, which opened in May 1721, at Nystad in Finland, with Osterman and Bruce again the Russian plenipotentiaries.

Peter refused to consider anything but minor concessions. He would not hear of yielding Viborg or Livonia. "No, I know my interests; if I leave Sweden now in Livonia, I would harbour a serpent in my bosom." No truce had been concluded, and in the summer 5,000 Russians were landed on the Swedish coast, who for the third time in three years spread devastation and terror. Thereat the Swedes gave in, and in September 1721 signed the treaty of Nystad. The war that Peter had begun twenty-one years earlier with ignominious rout was ended now in full triumph.

Peter had grown from an ardent, impetuous young man, with little knowledge of war or affairs of state though with great but unformed abilities, into the seasoned organizer of victory, the redoubtable and unchallenged ruler of a country which he had so harnessed that it now for the first time counted as a power in Europe. Sweden had fallen; Russia more than took her place. Her superiority in numbers and resources was immense, but this was of no avail without organization and leadership. Peter supplied both. Voltaire exaggerated but little when he wrote: "Pierre n'avait jamais fait la guerre qu'en politique, au lieu que Charles XII ne l'avait fait qu'en guerrier." As determined as Charles XII, but less obstinate; more fertile in combinations, more enriched by experience; as ruthless, but far less narrow; he laid the foundations of modern Russia, whilst Charles left his country in ruins.

He had begun by seeking to regain the old Russian coastal possessions at the head of the Gulf of Finland, the narrow strip of Ingria, a porthole on the sea. Now he ended by securing a great window to the west, all the Baltic coast from Riga round to Viborg. It was ice-bound in winter, but for a shorter period than Archangel, and it provided a far quicker route to Europe. At the beginning of the war Livonia was to go to Augustus of Poland, and so it was repeated in later treaties down to as late as 1711. But it was the Russians who had conquered unaided both Livonia and Estonia (1710), and, as has been seen, they remained in occupation and administration of these lands despite the protests of Augustus. Peter's losses in the south as a result of his disaster on the Pruth gave him additional reasons for requiring compensation in the north. From 1716 onwards he openly claimed both provinces, and when it came to parleys with Sweden he would not budge materially. All that could be extracted at Nystad was the payment of two million thalers and a qualified Swedish right to purchase Livonian grain duty free.

The acquisition of the Baltic provinces marked a new stage in the expansion of the empire. Another non-Russian region had been added to it, as had happened often before on the east, but the Baltic provinces were western, Lutheran, more advanced than Russia, and possessed of strong local institutions. They were not absorbed into the Russian administrative system, nor colonized by Russians. Nor did the Russian nobility receive lands there, a fact which told heavily against Peter in their eyes. The Baltic provinces lived apart under a species of autonomy, whereby the German upper class retained their position of dominance over the Lettish and Estonian subject population. The settlement made by Peter lasted, in most essentials, right down to the late nineteenth century. The result was that the German nobility flocked to court and into the army, navy, and civil departments, where they gave that uncorrupt and efficient service which Russia so greatly needed.

On the side of Finland, the treaty of Nystad secured to Peter Viborg and Karelia, which gave him control of Lake Ladoga, but he gave back the rest of Finland, in a pitiable condition of devastation. He had never claimed to keep it; with Kronstadt, Viborg, and Reval he accounted the defence of St. Petersburg assured. Only later in the century did the Russians hold that this was not so and that for the command of the Gulf of Finland they must hold its northern coast. Under Elizabeth they conquered and retained (1742) a small strip of territory protecting Viborg (where the frontier again runs to-day), but it was left to Alexander I, in the fourth war with Sweden within a century, to conquer and annex the whole of Finland (1808–9).

By one of the Nystad articles Peter expressly bound himself to interfere in no way whatever in the internal affairs of Sweden nor to attempt to change the succession. The death of Charles XII had been followed by a constitutional revolution which reduced the power of the crown to a shadow and substituted the rule of a parliamentary oligarchy. At the same time the Holstein claim to the throne was repudiated. Peter was only too willing that Sweden should become another Poland, and he had every intention of seeing that she remained so. He knew he could not at once impose the duke of Holstein on the Swedish throne, but the duke had taken refuge in Russia and Peter could use him to the full as a bugbear, for he had no other supporter and for the time being had lost to Denmark his contested lands in Schleswig. The long struggle in Sweden that was about to begin between the Caps and the Hats gave ample opportunities to Peter and his successors to circumvent the provisions of Nystad and utilize the duke for the advancement of Russian influence in Stockholm.

Inevitably and rightly the peace was received with

jubilation in Russia. Peter celebrated it with prolonged and prodigal festivities in his new capital. On the urgent pleading of the senate he accepted in great ceremony the titles of Father of his country, Peter the Great, and Emperor. He was declared to have led his subjects "from the darkness of ignorance on to the theatre of glory before the whole world and, so to speak, from non-existence to existence, and to have introduced them into the society of political peoples." For all the fulsome extravagance, there was a core of truth here. Peter had made Russia a power in Europe, and all three knew it. "By our deeds in war we have emerged from darkness into the light of the world, and those whom we did not know in the light now respect us." So Peter wrote some years earlier. A great Russian historian has summed up: "The steppe, eastern period of Russian history was ended; the maritime, western period was begun."

Chapter 7

Reform in Civil Government

ONE OF THE best known of the innumerable anecdotes about Peter recounts how, in anger at flattery of himself and belittlement of his father Alexis, he turned to prince Jacob Dolgoruky and asked his opinion, knowing that he would get a candid reply from "the Russian Cato." Dolgoruky answered that in respect of diplomacy and the navy Peter deserved more praise than his father; as regards the army and war, Alexis deserved great praise and Peter had done much, but the end of the struggle with Sweden would show whether he had done better than his father; as regards justice and internal order Alexis was superior, but if Peter were industrious he might surpass him. By 1721 he might claim to surpass his father, for he had both won the war with Sweden and proved his industry in the internal ordering of the state, and of the church as well.

Between 1718 and 1722 the central government was transformed by the refashioning of the senate and the creation of the procuratorship-general and the colleges in place of the old administrative departments; provincial and municipal governments were transformed; likewise the church by the creation of the synod in place of the patriarchate. These reforms in government were to a large extent long and carefully prepared and took three to four years to come fully into operation, but they were not thought out as a connected whole. Peter's approach still remained predominantly that of the artificer, not of the architect: his methods continued experimental and tentative.

He was the obverse of Speransky who a hundred years later drew up a comprehensive scheme of governmental reform for the empire of Alexander I. Whereas hardly anything of Speransky's closely articulated plan was carried into practice, the opposite was the case with Peter's

111

new institutions. Not only that: most of them continued in being for long, even if time and practice brought many alterations and a very different spirit in their working from that intended by their maker. The synod and the senate lasted, with various modifications, right down to 1917; the colleges and the procuratorship-general until the reign of Alexander I; the municipal reform until that of Catherine the Great.

The senate was originally created in 1711 to act in Peter's place when he departed for the war against Turkey, but it was continued as the chief executive organ of central government. Peter inherited from seventeenth-century Muscovy the council of magnates and a large number of departments of state (*cf.* p. 13). The former was already much decayed, and its place was taken by an un-systematized council of departmental ministers and Peter's special confidants. The departments lumbered along, with various regroupings and new creations, such as the ad-miralty. The pressure of war added greatly to the con-fusion and delays at the centre. Peter set up a new privy chancellery to control finance, and attempted to overcome the lack of effective central organization by his own super-abundant energy. In a characteristic letter to Catherine he unburdens thus: "I can't manage with my left hand, so with my right hand alone I have to wield both the sword and the pen; how many there are to help me, you know yourself."

By 1708 the situation was so critical that he decided on a sweeping measure of decentralization: the country was divided into eight (later ten) vast provincial governments, to which were allotted very wide powers, especially as regards revenue and all other sinews of war. The result was that the central departments were largely deprived of any effective power, and much of their work was trans-ferred to the governments.

It proved impossible to continue thus for long, and the senate was employed to fill the resultant void at the centre. It was to control the provincial governments, to be the head of the central administrative machine, to act as the highest court of justice, and especially "to collect money, as much as possible, for money is the artery of war." To this last end it had working under it the reconstructed privy chancellery and the chief "fiscal" (see p. 62), together with some five hundred "fiscals" in the provinces, the best-hated men in the country, who were charged with the secret police task of unearthing tax evasions and maladministration by officials.

The senate was so overburdened with work that it could not fail to be heavily in arrears and to function very badly, even apart from the failings of its individual members. These indeed were great. Two senators were convicted of gross peculation in the rigorous clean-up which Peter conducted in 1715: they escaped the death penalty, but were knouted, had their tongues cut out and suffered confiscation of their property. Such punishment of individuals— and other senators suffered later, though less severely— effected little real change. "I can turn dice," said Peter on one occasion, "not too badly with my chisel, but I cannot turn mules with my cudgel."

The senate was originally composed of nine members, whose decisions were to be unanimous (after 1714 by a majority). They worked together with great difficulty and great dilatoriness, and they quarrelled continually both with each other and with the all-powerful satraps at the head of the provinces, notably Menshikov, governor of St. Petersburg province, and Romadanovsky, the grim, bloodthirsty governor of Moscow. It was, above all, the failure of the senate in its vital financial tasks that drove Peter increasingly during these years to begin experimenting with colleges and the overhaul of government and taxation.

Colleges were much more than a new name for the old central departments of government. They involved, besides the organization of certain new departments, the absorption of almost all of the old departments in new bodies, which were to function, in accordance with carefully devised regulations and a fixed establishment, with boards at the head of each consisting of a president with ten others, acting by majority vote. They involved also recruitment of foreigners to start their working. There were originally nine colleges; foreign affairs, war, and admiralty; three dealing with finance; two dealing with economic affairs; finally, justice, which was as well the ministry of interior.

The colleges introduced a much more practical and rational division of labour at the centre, even though there still remained considerable overlapping of functions and numerous loose ends. For all their imperfections, they were undoubtedly a great improvement on the old confused and partially broken-down department system. Some steps had already been taken earlier towards such a redistribution of functions, and this aspect of the college reform system did not involve a serious clash with the past. The collegial board system, on the other hand, was in essentials quite new to Russia. It was a leading feature in the government of Sweden, Denmark, Prussia, and various other German states, and it appeared in an English form, for instance, in the Board of Admiralty and other boards. Peter had already borrowed much from the West, but never before had he borrowed institutions.[1]

Colleges were the fashion in northern Europe. Leibniz wrote to Peter: "There cannot be good administration except with colleges: their mechanism is like that of watches, whose wheels mutually keep each other in movement." The simile was exactly the kind to appeal to Peter. He was persuaded that the collegial system would prevent arbitrariness and promote orderly regularity; several heads were wiser than one; there would be less delay, less danger of dominance by one man, less likelihood of corruption. Something of the collegial system was imported, on paper, into parts of the provincial government, and for some four years before the General Regulation of 1720, which laid down in great detail the composition and functioning of the colleges, Peter had been preparing the way.

The Swedish colleges were taken as the main model, but much information was called for from others, notably

---

[1] Strictly speaking, the first institutional borrowings from the West were not the colleges but certain adaptations in provincial government (the *landrats* introduced in 1713 and copied from the Baltic provinces).

the Danes; "for we hear that the Swedes took from them." Peter did not intend to apply a slavish copy of these foreign institutions to the very different conditions of his own country. He constantly emphasized that they must be suitably adapted: "set out for my judgment those points in the Swedish regulations which are not good or inappropriate to the circumstances of this state." Even so, the regulations adopted represented a drastic change from accustomed ways and habits of thought. However, after changes made in 1722 when most of the foreigners were discharged, the new colleges took on many of the same characteristics as the old departments, and the collegial boards for the most part functioned, in fact, as the tools of their presidents.

The creation of the colleges relieved the senate of most of its detailed administrative work, leaving it free for general policy and the preparation of legislation, which latter task was increasingly devolved upon it by Peter. Further, the new justice college took over a great part of the judicial work of the senate, which became in the main confined to appellate jurisdiction. But it acted as the controlling agency over the colleges and remained the chief instrument of executive power, and it included, which it had not earlier, various of the most powerful men in the land, such as Menshikov and Tolstoi.

In 1722 Peter instituted a new office, that of the procurator-general, "our eye and attorney of state affairs," which became the most powerful single post in the empire. The procurator-general, though not himself a member of the senate, was to preside over that body (when Peter was not himself present, which he rarely was), to regulate its proceedings and to control its action. He was to watch over the functioning of the colleges through his own staff of procurators attached to each college. To him were subordinated the whole staff of "fiscals" throughout the country. In addition, he was given certain rights of initiating legislation.

The edict of 1722 establishing the procuratorship-general was worked on by Peter himself in great detail, and in contrast with his usual practice at this time was not referred to the senate. He appointed to this vitally important post Yaguzhinsky, the grasping, much-hated rival of Menshikov, like him raised up from nothing to the very top by Peter. He had undoubted capacities, and in particular three prerequisites for Peter's abiding favour, energy, decisiveness, and loyalty. During the previous ten years he had shown his ability for business in a variety of diplomatic and other missions, and had become one of Peter's most trusted boon-companions. He was well suited to inspire fear, but he was totally lacking in all the qualities of character and mind which were needed in a procurator-general, if the conceptions of good government towards which Peter was groping were to become realized in practice. Peter admitted that, though he had found a Turenne in war, he never found a Sully in governance.

The changes in central government—colleges, senate, procuratorship-general—were accompanied by changes in local government, by the laws on provincial (1719) and municipal (1721) government. The former swept away the ten vast governments of the 1708 reorganization and its later adjuncts, and created fifty provinces, subdivided into districts and endowed with an elaborate mechanism of chancelleries and offices. Of all Peter's reforms it kept the most closely to its Swedish model. It was far too schematic, too little adapted to Russian life, and too costly in money and men.

The most fundamental change attempted was the separation of justice and administration (1719). Eleven judicial districts were set up distinct from the provinces, and were placed under the control of the justice college, not of the local governors. This again was taken from Swedish practice, but it ran counter to the habit of looking on justice as a part of administration, which was engrained in Muscovite custom and practice. Very soon the local courts were being staffed by the local bureaucrats, and though some change of attitude was effected in the higher courts, the old Muscovite ways generally prevailed. The real separation of justice from administration was not effected until late in the nineteenth century, in the reign of Alexander II, and even then it was not complete.

Ever thinking first and foremost of the army, Peter subordinated the provincial government to its needs. Two of the most vital problems in the country were removed from the competence of the ordinary local authorities—the conscription levies and the new poll-tax. These were the affair of the regimental regions, into which Peter divided the empire for the purpose of quartering the army, and which cut across and overlapped with the provinces and districts and thus added a yet further element of complexity. The regimental regional offices were to work in conjunction with elected representatives of the landowners or taxpayers, but in practice the military dominated. Within a few years of Peter's death his elaborate system of provincial government was largely scrapped, and it was not until 1775 that Catherine the Great effected a lasting reorganization.

The municipal government law of 1721 involved less of a break with past custom, and in consequence much more of it subsisted in operation. It was to a large extent a remodelling of the 1699 municipal reform under the influence of borrowing from the West; in this case, in accordance with Peter's instructions, mainly from Riga and Reval. In each town the merchants, manufacturers, traders, and skilled artisans were organized in two guilds, according to their wealth, and the whole business of administration, justice, and economic development in the towns was entrusted to elected bodies from these guilds. They were dominated by the handful of rich merchant-traders and controlled by a new college in St. Petersburg, called the chief magistracy. In fact, the power of the chief magistracy soon stifled any local independence, and Peter's aim of encouraging the growth of a self-reliant, public-spirited middle class in the towns was almost entirely stultified.

The all-round reorganization of government that has just been sketched was effected during the war, and it bore many of the marks of Peter's incessant struggle for the resources wherewith to wage war. At the same time, however, the later reforms reflect a broadening in Peter's outlook and a changed realization of the functions of the state, of the meaning of good government, and of the importance of institutions. Whereas earlier he had thought in terms of persons and immediate, hand-to-mouth measures to cope with this or that crisis or need, in these later years of his life he began to take longer views and to supplement impulsive decisions with carefully formulated and long-meditated measures.

He had begun with not much more aim than "to preserve internal tranquillity, to defend the state from external attack and by every means to improve and extend trade" (1702). These always remained for him paramount objects, but by 1720 he had added "justice and police, that is justice in the courts and citizenship." He no longer contented himself with curt, cryptic edicts ordering that such and such be done at once under direst pains; "edicts written as though with the knout" (Pushkin). The major enactments that began with the army regulations of 1716 were prefaced with explanations of the need for the legislation in question, historical parallels, and appeals to reason and utility. The subjects of the Russian state, of which Peter was the first servitor, were instructed and argued with, not merely commanded from on high.

Peter's own share in these major enactments was greater than is often allowed. The rôle of his personal chancellery, headed by Makarov, always at hand, was central. The work involved in the elaboration of these measures was very large and was spread over a number of years. Naturally this was done by others; but the initial impulsion, much of the selection of material and of the revision of drafts, and the final decisions were his own handiwork. As would be expected, the army regulations of 1716, and the navy regulations that followed in 1720, owed almost everything to Peter himself.

In his last years, the emphasis on "justice and police" marks a new trend. Peter had imbibed in the German lands something of the terminology and ideas made fashionable there by Pufendorff and others, ideas which became known as cameralism and which set great store on police. This was a word used not in our restricted sense but with the meaning of "the science governing the various occupations according to the purposes of the state," as a later definition runs. In the preparation of the legislation for the colleges and local and municipal government Peter made especial use of two Germans, Fick from Holstein and Luberas from Silesia, both of them well acquainted with German and Swedish thought and practice in administration. Leibniz, amongst others, added his quota of memoranda. Under these influences Peter introduced into Russia such expressions as "the interest of the state," "the general good," "universal national service." From these same sources came the conception that Russia should be "a police state," "a regulated state," a state governed in accordance with rule and precept, not with custom and caprice.

What this "police state" might be is best illustrated from the law of 1721 creating the new college to deal with municipal affairs. Police is described as "the soul of citizenship and of all good order and the fundamental support of civil security and propriety." Police "contributes to rights and justice; gives birth to good order and morals, gives security to all against robbers, thieves, ravishers, counterfeiters and suchlike; drives away disorderly and dissolute living and compels everyone to labour and honourable occupation; makes for good economy and careful and good service; maintains towns and streets; prevents high prices and assures all needful supplies; guards against disease; keeps streets and buildings clean; forbids domestic extravagance and all manifest transgressions; takes care of beggars, the poor and sick, outcasts and other indigent persons; protects widows and orphans and foreigners, according to divine command; educates the young in purity and chasteness and good apprenticeship."

Thus, the word "police" meant not merely what we now call the police, but much of what we call the social services, as well as various economic and financial functions, and even in addition something radically different from all these tasks of the state or local bodies, namely the spirit of law-abidingness and membership in a community.

Another attempt of the same kind was made in the 1719 provincial government reform, in which were included, unlike the Swedish model to which it otherwise so closely conformed, duties covering a wide variety of health, educational, and economic schemes. Lack of local initiative and lack of money prevented practical results, and such generalities remained almost entirely on the paper on which they were written. Peter had few illusions as to their being translated into practice in his own day. Nevertheless, these aspirations well illustrate his ideal of enlightened despotism, and they are a foretaste of much that is best in Russian social thought and striving in the latter part of the eighteenth century.

Only a handful of the younger men he had trained up, his "fledglings," were imbued with devotion not merely to the person of their "father," but as well to his ideal of honest, efficient service to their country. Almost all his leading men and in general the class of landowners on which the working of his reforms depended failed him. He could not prevent extortion, corruption, and embezzlement, often on a gigantic scale. The new men that he raised from nothing were as bad as, or in the case of Menshikov worse than, the old type of magnates or gentry who were accustomed to regard government posts as their lucrative perquisites. The senators only too frequently incurred their master's deserved castigation for behaving (as he wrote) "like chaffering market-women instead of counsellors of state." Their personal rivalries and violent brawls added to the confusion and delay at the top.

Away in the country, the serf-owners were intent on controlling their estates for their own benefit, and cared little or nothing for Peter's attempts to link them up with provincial government in public-spirited betterment of the country's resources. Both at the centre and on the circumference the army of officials failed, save in rare cases, to imitate their master's sense of duty to the state. "The tsar pulls uphill alone with the strength of ten, but millions pull downhill." Administration remained as before "a gainful business." This, together with fear of punishment, were the two most powerful incentives. The essential was to fulfil an order in such a way as to avoid punishment by one's superiors.

The constraint of fear operated not only on officials, but on all classes. It was nothing new; as has been seen earlier (pp. 13–14), it was a glaring feature of Muscovite government. Peter, both by his own irascible tempestuousness and by emphatic iteration in his edicts, made punishment still appear one of the chief means of government. He would laud the example of Ivan the Terrible. If a field is overflowing with weeds, it must be purged with fire before wheat is sown. He spared neither high nor low; a governor of Siberia could be executed, a chief "fiscal" broken on the wheel alive.

In Peter's eyes the crying evil of Russia was non-observance of law. At its worst it was a matter of sheer banditry, on the prevalence of which his repeated edicts give ample testimony. He himself declared: "Nothing is so necessary to the administration of a state as the strict observance of civil laws, since it is vain to write laws when they are not observed or are played with like cards, suit matched against suit, which nowhere in the world happened so much as used to be with us, and in part still is, and very great care is needed to put all persons under the fortress of justice." How to translate these maxims into practice was beyond Peter. His own personality and way of life told against him. Masterful and dominating, accustomed from his youth up to use his fists, his famous oaken cudgel, or on occasion his sword against his closest advisers, he could rule his subjects, but could not permeate government with a new spirit.

Peter acted in all spheres of his unbounded energy through compulsion, the compulsion of his wholly exceptional will-power in alliance with the traditional power of the tsar. This compulsion took both the negative (and equally traditional) form of punishment and the positive, novel form of trying to force his subjects to acquire new habits by doing this or that in such-and-such a way in accordance with his own prescription. While he wanted Russians to stand on their own feet and assume responsibility for themselves, while he wanted them to serve the fatherland with the same assiduous devotion as himself, his own overwhelming personality and his increasing fits of unbridled passion created an atmosphere that was the least favourable to the growth of civic sense and public justice which in his legislation he attempted to inculcate.

On the one hand, he would write: "According to these orders act, act, act. I won't write more, but you will pay with your head if you interpret orders again." On the other hand, he would inveigh against excessively cautious interpretation of instructions: "This is as if a servant, seeing his master drowning, would not save him until he had satisfied himself as to whether it was written down in his contract that he should pull him out of the water." He required his servants at one and the same time to be his slaves and to be free men acting for themselves. The combination of despotism and freedom, enlightenment and serfdom, was a circle that could not be squared.

Characteristically, in his efforts "to pull all persons under the fortress of justice," Peter relied in fact not so much on the procuratorship-general or other new institutions set up by his legislation, but on his trusted guards officers. These became in the latter part of the reign something like *missi dominici*, charged by the sovereign in person with special commissions overriding the ordinary governmental routine. The guards were drawn from the landowning families, but they served for life and had been brought up in the full spate of Peter's reforms. They had grown to manhood unhabituated to the traditional Muscovite ways, and were, for the most part, ardent supporters and admirers of their creator, who never failed to care for their interests and give scope to their abilities.

Peter used the guards more and more frequently on all manner of extraordinary, non-military missions, notably to bring to book those in high authority. Provincial governors were coerced into the performance of their duties, disputes even between senators settled through guards officers picked for the purpose. The most important state trials of the highest officials were conducted by special courts that included the indispensable guards. The government of the Ukraine was controlled (1722) by a guards brigadier and six staff officers. Their official appellation, "compellers," speaks volumes. In earlier years Peter used them in the army to compel other troops to discipline; now in his closing years he used them in government to compel authorities, high and low alike, to behave themselves and carry out the law. They were, as it were, a personal extension of Peter's own thunderclap will.

Necessarily, such agents even of a ruler as effectively autocratic as Peter could only act relatively spasmodically. Here and there they could mitigate bureaucratic evils or incompetence, jolt forward the clumsy mechanism, or bring to justice scandalous provincial potentates. They could be no substitute for Peter's conception of a "regulated state." Yet for a century and a half every ruler of Russia found it invaluable to follow Peter's practice in his use of the guards. Yet more; for exactly a hundred years from Peter's death the guards decided either the accession or the maintenance on the throne of every empress or emperor.

Chapter 8

Religion and Reform

THE REFORMS OF PETER in civil government were paralleled by reforms in the church and the creation of the synod (1721) in place of the patriarchate. His own personal attitude to religion is hard to estimate. He has been accused of "protestant indifferentism." He certainly took a lively, though intermittent, interest when abroad in western forms of the Christian religion, and the attitude of the Lutheran churches to the state and the duties of the citizen was one which appealed to him. He was Erastian and anti-ritualist, but except for the adoption of the collegial principle in the synod, there is no definite evidence that either his own beliefs or his ecclesiastical policy were specifically influenced by western conceptions. What may in general be true of his attachment to the West is that he thereby "rubb'd off the rust of that bigotry to his . . . own religion, which his people seem generally to have contracted," as an English chaplain in Russia wrote of him.

Peter was brought up as a child along traditional Orthodox lines, with a good knowledge of the Bible and of the liturgy and with an aptitude for church singing. In his middle years he did what he could to spread abroad in Russia a good text of the Bible, and to the end of his days he would on occasion push forward and take charge of a choir in singing—absurd, transitory metamorphosis, yet in keeping with one who was ever the practitioner, never the onlooker. While he broke loose from the traditional round of religious ceremonial that encrusted the tsars of Muscovy, he continued normal religious observances, and he endowed his new capital with a monastery on a lavish scale, named after Alexander Nevsky, the medieval victor over the Swedes almost on the same spot.

Throughout his life he accepted with conviction the belief in the omnipotence of God instilled into him as a boy. He was at one with his subjects in seeing the hand of

God in all things, great and small, good and evil: history with all its ups and downs was the working out of God's will. But he was at odds with the majority of his subjects in their practical corollaries of fatalistic resignation, devotion to the outward forms of worship, and ingrained superstition. In Peter's eyes man was responsible to his Maker, none more so than the tsar himself: duty to God involved duty to one's neighbour, the active combating of evil and the development of the faculties with which God had endowed His creatures, in particular the gift of reason.

Secular and rationalist by taste, Peter recked little of the subtleties of theological speculation and nothing of the lonely struggle of the human soul for grace and redemption. He practised a mundane gospel of work for the honour and glory of God, with which were conveniently identified the strength, prosperity, and orderliness of Russia. For him the two cardinal sins were hypocrisy and laziness; hypocrisy, against which he wished that there had been added an eleventh commandment; laziness "which [according to Holy Writ] is the mother of all evil," most notably of ignorance.

Peter usually approached religious problems, as he did other problems, without theorizing or elaborate calculation. He himself made no play with the idea of the divine right of kings, though his principal ecclesiastical henchman drew copiously on Byzantine theory and practice and even on ancient Rome to justify the indefeasible preeminence of the tsar as *pontifex maximus*. He regarded the throne as a trust conferred on him by God, to whom alone he was accountable. Good government required good subjects, God-fearing and therefore tsar-fearing, believing in the essentials of the Christian faith and the sanctity of the moral code. Such belief and corresponding action depended largely on the teaching and example of the clergy. Hence the church was an indispensable instrument in governance.

The consequence of this outlook was that Peter, in fact, required the subordination of the church to his conception of right governance, and this involved continual struggles with most of the monks and clergy. He was in any case involved in struggle with the schismatics, who regarded him as Anti-Christ and the official church as apostate. As has been pointed out earlier (pp. 20–24), the Muscovy that Peter inherited was deeply divided on religious and cultural issues. The division was accentuated both by his manner of life and by his public actions.

His conception of right governance involved borrowing from the West; this was repellent to devout churchmen and schismatics alike, with the exception of a handful of the higher ecclesiastics. It involved a large measure of toleration of other Christian religions; this was widely viewed with alarm and disgust. It involved reform both of the monasteries and of the secular clergy; this was opposed by most, though not by the best, of both sections of the ecclesiastics. It involved, in the end, the abolition of the patriarchate and its replacement by the synod; this was in general unpopular, and was felt by many to be tantamount to further subjection of the church to the state, but it did not arouse deep antagonism. On the other hand, Peter's conception of right governance did not involve any change in ritual, still less in dogma, or in the position of the Orthodox church as the established state religion.

A modified tolerance of Catholics and Protestants had been an unpopular feature of the regency of Sophia. Peter, with his widespread and continuous recruiting of foreigners, had no hesitation in extending such toleration on grounds of state policy. Nor was he alarmed by the spread among Russians of small circles of Protestant sectaries. In the conquered Baltic provinces the Lutheran religion was effectively guaranteed its dominant position. He was even prepared in some circumstances to tolerate the Old Believers, if there was any chance of gain thereby. When confronted with certain colonies of Old Believers in the iron-works district of Olonets in the far north, he was prepared to let them be, provided that they could supply good iron-workers—which they did. "Let them believe what they will," he said, "for if reason cannot turn them from their superstition, neither fire nor sword can do it. It is foolish to make them martyrs. They are unworthy of the honour, and would not in this way be of use to the state."

He was, in general, less inclined to persecute the Old Believers for their religious conservatism than many of the church leaders. Since, however, the line between religious conservatism and political opposition was exceedingly narrow, the great majority of the Old Believers and the sectarians who grew out of them fared very badly at Peter's hands. They were subjected to double taxation, special dress regulations, and a large number of discriminatory disabilities.

From the first the two facts that struck Peter most were the ignorance of the clergy and the wealth of the hierarchy and the larger monasteries. He was anxious to take steps for education, but in fact he left it to the individual initiative of a few energetic bishops. As usual, war was his paramount concern. His first action was not to build church schools, but to melt down the church bells to replenish his artillery lost at Narva. His second action was to drain off the very large revenues of the church into the coffers of the state. In all, the church lands were computed to include almost one-fifth of the peasantry. Pushing much further attempts made half a century earlier by his father, he revived (1701) a secular department of monasteries which controlled their lands, to the advantage of the poorer monasteries but especially to the advantage of his treasury. Later, the great estates of the patriarchate and of the episcopate were similarly controlled. In addition, the church was deprived of a large part of its profitable jurisdiction.

For more than two centuries the question of church and especially monastic landholding had been a contentious issue. Peter was not embarking on a wholly new policy, and he had support both from the laity and from a group of patriotic, reforming bishops; but inevitably within the church antagonism was bitterly accentuated. The lay power was usurping the rights of the spiritual power and seemed likely to go to the length of expropriating all the lands of the church. In fact, however, Peter refrained from such a measure, and it was left for Catherine the Great to take this step in 1764.

Meanwhile the patriarchate remained vacant. Peter knew two patriarchs, each of them ignorant ultraconservatives. They, like the bishops, were appointed by the tsar from three candidates put forward by the synod of bishops. As had been the invariable custom of the Russian church, only monks could be appointed. When the patriarch Adrian died in 1700, Peter had no satisfactory successor to hand, and he was absorbed in the struggle with Charles XII. He drifted into the policy of leaving the patriarchate vacant. An acting patriarch was appointed in the person of Stephen Yavorsky, a well-educated, upright Ukrainian monk, with a gift of eloquence and a disposition to reform.

The church in the Ukraine, with its higher cultural standard and its wider horizon, had already been influencing the church in Muscovy for the last forty years, and Peter found here men who could raise the level of the Muscovite clergy and were in sympathy with much at least in his reforming ideas. Yavorsky worked well with Peter for some years, but, as he said himself, he was better fitted to rule a monastery than to preside over a church with so imperious a sovereign. The two men drew further and further apart, and Yavorsky did not hide his sympathies with the tsarevich Alexis.

Peter transferred his hopes to another Ukrainian, Theophan Prokopovich, a highly intellectual man of great ambition and energy, varied gifts and much knowledge of Rome and the West (including Protestantism, with which he had a certain sympathy). Peter raised him to high position as the chief propagandist of his ideas, and from 1718 onwards turned his mind to a new ordering of the church. The outcome was the publication in 1721 of the "Spiritual Regulation," a lengthy document prepared by Prokopovich and carefully revised by Peter, which initiated a whole programme of reform and set up a new body at the head of the church, the "Holy Governing Synod," a title devised by Peter himself.

The synod was to take the place of the patriarch and deal with "all the affairs of which the patriarchs had heretofore direction." This included the administration of the immense estates of the patriarchate and its dependent monasteries, which between them were estimated to possess nearly forty thousand male serfs. In addition, it was given control of all the other (far larger) church and monastic lands, and had jurisdiction in all ecclesiastical and religious matters. It was granted the power of revising the "Spiritual Regulation," but not without the emperor's consent.

The synod was formed on the same model as the colleges, composed of a president, vice-president, and eight other members, appointed by Peter from the clergy, both secular and regular. It was, however, superior to any of the colleges, and Peter intended it to be co-equal with the senate. Like the senate, it had a chief-procurator, a layman, appointed of course by the emperor, to watch over its business. Long subsequently this official became notorious as virtually the imperial minister of religion. The adoption of the collegial principle was the one indubitably western element in Peter's reform of the church, but the creation of the synod itself as the highest body in the autocephalous Orthodox church in Russia was not wholly an innovation, since in some respects it could link on with what had been the practice before the metropolitan of Moscow was created patriarch in 1589.

Although the patriarchate had existed in Muscovy for not much more than a century, it occupied an exceptional and overtopping position, and during that period it had been filled by two outstanding men who made the patriarch the equal or even the superior of the tsar; Philaret (1619–33), the father of the first of the Romanov dynasty, Michael, and the real ruler of Muscovy during his reign, and Nikon (1652–66) who had lorded it over Peter's father, Alexis, and raised the claims of the patriarchate to such a pitch that he was deprived of his office by a Church Council (see above, pp. 21–22). None of his successors repeated such extreme claims, and it was unlikely that another Nikon would find his way to the patriarchate and challenge as directly the authority of the tsar.

Yet the reactionary attitude of the last two patriarchs

might, if repeated, be all the more dangerous when, as Peter well knew, so many of his subjects wished for nothing better than riddance from his rule and a lead backwards to accustomed ways and less onerous days. Thus, Peter explicitly justifies the abolition of the patriarchate on the ground that the vulgar look on the patriarch "as a second sovereign, equal in power to the autocrat himself, or even above him," so that it is possible for ambitious clerics and seditious men to incite the commonalty against the sovereign; "what then if furthermore the chief pastor himself is puffed up with a great opinion of himself and will not rest quiet? 'Tis hard to describe what calamities ensue therefrom," as can be seen from the history of Byzantium and the papacy, "to say nothing of the like agitations that have been formerly amongst ourselves."

Peter abolished the patriarchate and substituted for it the synod after consultation with the hierarchy but without summoning a Church Council, such as Muscovy was accustomed to, and without prior agreement with the other Orthodox churches. He had come to have a poor opinion of the other Orthodox patriarchs, as also of the Phanariote Greeks at the head in Constantinople. Inevitably they acquiesced in the change in Russia without serious demur, since Russia was the only independent country with an Orthodox church and there could be no question of challenging her autocephalous position. The synod simply took the place of the patriarch of Moscow *vis-à-vis* the four other patriarchs. Together with the senate, it proved to be the most long lasting of Peter's new institutions, though with various modifications in its competence and functioning. Only with the fall of the Romanov dynasty in 1917 was it abolished and the patriarchate restored.

The setting up of the synod certainly weakened the position of the church as against the state, but it is worth noticing that Peter, unlike Henry VIII, did not assume the title of the "Head of the Church." That title was not used until 1797 by the emperor Paul. For Peter it was quite sufficient to adopt the style "supreme defender and protector of the doctrines of the prevailing faith and guardian of orthodoxy and all good order in Holy

Church." The term cæsaro-papism, so often used in the West both of the Byzantine and the Russian empires, had better be avoided. Whatever may be said of some of Peter's theoreticians, Peter himself avoided raising the most contentious issues of principle and was content to rely on the well-worn scriptural maxims enjoining the obedience of subjects to their rulers. He provided for disputes over competence between church and state to be handled by joint conference of synod and senate. A few such conferences were held, but the practice soon lapsed. In fact, since the synod was an ecclesiastical committee, appointed by the sovereign, and not a free synod of the clergy or of the church as a whole, and since it was endowed with very centralized powers over the church, it came to suffer mainly from bureaucratic complexity and remoteness: it became itself fused, to a large extent, with the lay power, rather than dominated by that power.

Throughout Russian history the relationship of the secular and spiritual powers had never been specifically defined, and the struggle with Nikon had not resulted in any precise theoretical formulation. Until that struggle the Muscovite church and state had usually worked together in close harmony. The issues raised in the sixteen-sixties were not those of clear-cut opposition of church to state, but, on the contrary, divergent and conflicting issues between the tsar, patriarch, and official church against the Old Believers, and between the patriarch, standing in the end almost alone, against the tsar supported by most of the church. The victory of Alexis over Nikon was at the same time a victory for the church against domination by the patriarch. Thus Peter did not have to face a patriarchate that had made good claims to supremacy within the church, let alone claims as against the state.

This fact helps to explain why Peter did not meet with more direct and effective opposition in his dealings with the church. Further, the Orthodox were divided among themselves: not only were the Old Believers divided from the official church, which itself needed the support of the state against them, but there was much division between the "white" clergy, the seculars who were married, and the "black," the regulars who were not, and from whom alone bishops could be chosen. While the church as a whole was wealthy, the great majority of the parish priests were miserably poor. In addition, the upper ecclesiastics, both "black" and "white," were themselves divided. By the latter part of Peter's reign a fair number of them were appointees of his, and on the whole represented an energetic reforming element. This was particularly true of the newcomers from the Ukraine, though their origin gave rise to much hostility. Finally, no churchman arose with a strong personality and great spiritual gifts who could act as a leader to galvanize the widespread but divergent currents of opposition to Peter within the church. He had, too, the further advantage that, while some of his measures were intensely distasteful to the great bulk of the Orthodox, others of his measures were designed to grapple with acknowledged evils within the church.

In conjunction with the synod, Peter set on foot reforms directed towards enforcing ecclesiastical discipline, overhauling the monasteries, and improving the standards of the secular clergy. There were computed to be over 14,000 monks and over 10,000 nuns, something like three times the number in England at the time of the dissolution of the monasteries. It was easy to find instances of great laxity in many of the smaller monasteries, as well as in some of the larger. Their contribution to education and learning was, on the whole, small. Their charity, in Peter's eyes, had too often degenerated into the upkeep of swarms of ne'er-do-well vagrants, who incurred the special wrath of Peter, "hale and lazy beggars . . . enemies to God . . . useless hands."

Peter, with his lack of any true understanding of the monastic ideal and with his disgust at what he considered to be its too frequent parody in the Russia of his day, might have been expected to deal with the monasteries as did Henry VIII in England. He spoke of the greater part of the monks being "parasites," given over to idleness and superstition. "The order of monks," he wrote, "was antiently a kind of mirror to the Christian religion, and the pattern for repentance and good discipline; but it is now the reverse, and the origin of infinite disorders and disturbances." Yet he did not proceed to sweep the monasteries away. In the then state of Russia such a measure would have overbrimmed the cup, and there is no evidence that he ever considered so deeply unpopular an amputation. Edicts were issued drastically limiting the intake of monks, enforcing residence and discipline, closing monasteries with less than thirty members and using their buildings for parish churches or schools. No new monasteries or nunneries were to be founded without permission of the synod. Encouragement was given to monastic schools, hospitals, and almshouses, especially for Peter's favourites, his army veterans.

To education Peter gave in his last years increasingly more systematic attention. "For learning is good and fundamental, and as it were the root, the seed, and first principle of all that is good and useful in church and state." As regards the education of the clergy, it was to the bishops rather than to the monasteries (apart from their revenues) that Peter mainly looked. In several dioceses a number of schools for priests' sons, free of charge, had been successfully started some years earlier. The synod now required every bishop to do likewise, and by 1725 forty-six such schools had been opened, with a liberal curriculum and with teachers drawn from the resuscitated Slavonic-Greek-Latin academy in Moscow. Much remained merely on paper, and as in the other Petrine schools education was conceived of as a form of state service: that was what was meant by calling learning "the first principle of all that is good and useful in church and state." Schools were run as if they were barracks; desertion from school was relatively as frequent as desertion from the army, and was punished accordingly. Nevertheless, the diocesan schools developed later in the century into really valuable instruments of education, not only for priests' sons but for the provincial laity. This aspect of Peter's church reforms links on with the general question of his attitude to education and cultural change, which in turn was part and parcel of his outlook on social and economic policy.

Chapter 9

Social and Economic Change

IN THESE SAME YEARS (1718–24) during which Peter remodelled so much in church and state, he likewise left his most lasting marks on the social and economic development of his country. When he came to the throne, Russia, despite much regional variation, was predominantly a land of serfdom, in which the right to own land and serfs was confined to a small upper class, who in return owed service. When he died, broadly speaking the same was true. So far from attempting to alter serfdom as the basis of the state, Peter clamped it down more firmly on the peasantry. But at the same time he imposed on the landowners the duty of service to the state to an extent never attempted by his predecessors and in forms that were new.

It has been pointed out in the opening chapter (p. 14) that the landowning class was much differentiated within itself, but its members were in two respects alike: they alone (together with the church) could own serfs, and they all owed service to the state. Their service was in the main military, but in the course of the seventeenth century enforcement of it had become lax. Peter shrank from nothing in making a reality of service. The landowners must not only fight, they must know how to. Peter's adoption of western military technique and his creation of a fleet involved a completely new training and the learning of the very rudiments of new skills. He and his subjects—above all the landowners, the officer and directing class—must go to school to the West. They must learn from foreign experts brought to Russia, and they must learn by going abroad to train. Hence the "great embassy" of 1697 (see pp. 36–42), and the hiring of more and more foreigners for technical service and the giving of instruction.

From that time onwards Peter was continually sending

to the West batches of young Russians for apprenticeship in this or that branch of military or naval science, not for education in the broad sense. Later, indeed, their studies became wider, and were not so exclusively concerned with such subjects as navigation or gunnery, while from the first apprenticeship abroad involved, at any rate, some learning of foreign languages. Yet to the end of his life Peter looked on education as a training for some specific form of state service: if men went abroad to learn economics, it was for the sake of his new tariff; if they were trained in languages, it was in order to act as translators or to serve as diplomats. Education was simply the first rung in the ladder of state service.

The men thus sent abroad were mostly young and predominantly from the landowning class, including a number from the very highest families. Most were paid by the state small sums, usually in arrears. Many were "volunteers," whether nominally or actually, but later on education abroad became a state assignment. Similarly, at home Peter attempted to make education obligatory for the children of the landowners. At first it was not so. The "navigation school," started by Farquharson in 1701, and the "cipher schools" which followed, were voluntary, and were open to all classes, not to the landowners only. These secular schools, the first of their kind in Russia, were very unsatisfactory and very narrow, concentrating almost exclusively on elementary mathematics. Still, they were a beginning, and Peter, with his usual sanguine peremptoriness, had no hesitation in decreeing (1714) that this very slim foundation was to be expanded at once to serve for the compulsory elementary education of the children of all landowners and civil servants from the ages of ten to fifteen. The penalty for non-observance of the edict was as novel as the edict itself—without a school-leaving certificate none of them could marry.

The landowners retaliated virtually with a boycott, and two years later Peter accepted defeat and revoked the edict. Instead, the children of the gentry were to go to three new schools in St. Petersburg, of a superior sort and confined to the gentry. The character and purpose of these schools were evident from their names—Naval Academy, Engineering Academy, and Artillery Academy. With these Peter had some success in his efforts to impose education on the landowning class, but it was not until his niece, the empress Anna, founded in 1730 the Corps of Pages on an exclusive, aristocratic basis that Peter's frail plant took root.

His "cipher schools," languishing from the very start, were curtailed in 1722, and soon afterwards gave place to special schools for the children of garrison troops and to others run by the Admiralty for technical education. Thus Peter's original conception of compulsory elementary education for the landowners in all-class schools foundered almost from the start, partly through his own hasty lack of preparation, partly through the reluctance or refusal of parents to submit their sons to this new form of service.

The old form of service in the army was bad enough, now that there was a standing war; and worse still now that service in the navy was also laid upon their shoulders. The army brought some rewards, above all in the guards, but the navy none, and it remained universally and intensely unpopular. The third form of service, in the civil departments, was more lucrative and far less onerous, and consequently more attractive. In the end (1722) Peter came to a rationing system, whereby the military forces were allotted two-thirds and the civilian offices one-third of the landowners entering state employment.

If Peter in the main failed in his attempt at compulsory education for the landowners, he was to a large extent successful in enforcing their compulsory service. The old service registers were revised and kept up to date; frequent musters were held of the young gentry, sometimes even up to the age of thirty; drastic measures were taken against "those who buried themselves in their villages" or "did not present themselves through stiff-necked sloth." In his determination to root out the provincial landowners from their easy-going, family nests and drive them to service and "to seek their own bread," Peter even went to the length of a frontal attack on the ancient Muscovite law of inheritance, according to which immovable property was equally divided among the sons of the deceased. This practice had indeed led to great subdivision of estates and to much impoverishment of the lesser gentry. He had long had in mind some measure against this, and in 1714 he issued an edict establishing a species of entail totally foreign to existing custom and practice, whereby immovable property of all kinds could not be sold and was to be inherited by one son, or, if there were no sons, by one daughter or one relation.

So radical a change in disposal of property and in family habits could not fail to meet with antagonism and obstruction. It applied equally to burghers and to landowners, but it was aimed especially at the latter. Even though they found easy loopholes for evasion, the edict of 1714 remained one of their most insistent charges against Peter, and they were not satisfied until they secured its annulment in 1730.

His failure here is in striking contrast with his success in a second legal measure, intimately affecting the landowners' interests, whereby he converted what had been revertible service fiefs into hereditary estates. The reason is simple: Peter in acting thus was but giving legal sanction to what had been for long becoming a living, social fact. Again, the failure of his entail law is in striking contrast with his success in remodelling the service conditions of the landowning class through a graded hierarchy of military and civil ranks, known as the table of ranks (1722).

By the table of ranks military posts were divided from civil, and all officers or officials were classified in fourteen parallel grades. Through each of these it was necessary to pass, beginning from the bottom, just as it had been Peter's practice to make his guards officers, like himself, start from the ranks. Promotion from grade to grade was to be partly by length of service and partly by exceptional merit. Standing in the state service took precedence of birth, even in the court and social hierarchy. The privileges of the landowning class, notably those of owning serfs and of being exempt from the poll-tax, were extended hereditarily to all persons, whether Russians or foreigners, who reached the eighth grade, and in the case of the army and navy even from the lowest grade.

Throughout his life Peter picked men for multifarious duties without regard to birth or class, and he now made legislative provision for a wide opening of the door into the privileged ranks of the landowning class, in the interests of recruitment for military or state service. From this time forward the landowning class began to receive an influx of newcomers, who in the course of the next two generations broadened its composition and changed its complexion. It became a major object of the old landowning class to set a stop to this influx. Already in Peter's youth the old aristocratic families were complaining about low-born newcomers being thrust into office and command: throughout his reign the process was being accelerated; now at its close it received legal definition.

Despite subsequent alterations, the table of ranks had a profound influence on the future. It set the stamp on the hierarchical, bureaucratic ordering of the upper class in military and state service, which during the next two centuries became so prominent a feature of the social structure of Russia. Rank, in the sense of position in the table of ranks, largely displaced birth or wealth in the administrative and social scale.

Whereas Peter's entail law had been imposed by his sudden fiat, without any preliminary steps preparing the way, his table of ranks gave final form to a pattern which had been increasingly taking shape during his whole reign. This was one main reason why the law of 1722 was effective. Further, the separation of military from civil ranks, which was one of the most important features of the table of ranks, did not come as a bolt from the blue; it had already been mooted forty years before at the time of the abolition of the old Muscovite code of precedence (see p. 14). Finally, the edict putting into force the table of ranks, although it owed much to western parallels and reeked of German titles, was not as it were launched upon Russia from abroad: it was not issued until after twelve months of consultation between Peter, the senate, and certain of the colleges. The fact is indicative of the change, already noted previously, in his methods of legislation.

While Peter reorganized and broadened the landowning class on the basis of compulsory service, he laid even heavier burdens upon the peasantry and extended the bonds of serfdom. By a number of piecemeal measures, culminating in the poll-tax at the very end of his reign, he consolidated developments that had been growing under his predecessors, whereby the variegated, fluctuating composition of the peasantry was becoming hardened and shaped to the needs both of the landowners, ever eager for more serfs and tighter control over them, and of the government, ever in search of more and more revenue. The gradually disappearing distinction between slaves (never a large class) and serfs was abolished. Thereby the condition of the former was somewhat improved, but the state gained in that the previous slaves now became taxpayers and liable to military service, which they had not been previously.

With the same object of enforcing services or taxes on all classes of his subjects, Peter did his utmost to ascribe to serfdom or to bring within his financial net the motley, intermediate class of free labourers, engaged partly in handicrafts, partly in vagrant, casual labour and transport, and partly as dependants of churches and monasteries. Another large group of the peasantry, the state peasants, were subjected to conditions nearly amounting to serfdom, and for some of them a new and onerous obligation was added, that of compulsory seasonal work in Peter's new factories and mines, especially in the iron- and copper-works. In addition, a new type of serfdom was established in the shape of the permanent attachment of certain villages as labour for these works.

For the serfs of the landowners, who constituted the bulk of the peasantry, the reign of Peter marked a further stage in their almost complete subjection to the will of their masters. In his eyes, just as the landowner was to be tied to service, the townsman to his trade or handicraft, so the peasant was to be tied to the land. Many of his particular edicts on the peasantry merely gave sanction to what was already customary or becoming so. Though a few of them sought to mitigate the arbitrary power of the serf-owners, yet the general effect of Peter's legislation was to strengthen their position as little rulers of their estates, endowed with rights of jurisdiction and punishment and with control over the movement of their serfs through the new requirement (1722) that no serf should move from his master's estate without his written permission. Thus Peter was the originator of the passport system which developed throughout imperial Russia and, in much-changed form, is applied in the Soviet Union.

He left also a lasting imprint on most classes of the peasantry, as well as on the townsfolk, by his new recruiting regulations and his new poll-tax to meet the needs of his new standing army. Peter was at war continuously for twenty-eight years, from 1695 to 1723, first against Turkey, then against Sweden, finally against Persia. The devouring maw of the army and navy swallowed up over three-quarters of the revenue already in 1701, four-fifths in 1710, and even at the end of his reign more than two-thirds. When he came to the throne in 1682, military expenditure absorbed more than half the revenue, and meanwhile throughout his reign Peter was voraciously extracting more and more from his subjects in taxation.

He fought all his wars through the unaided toil of his own people: no foreign loans were raised. The whole weight fell on one generation: no internal loans were floated. Loans, banks, and paper money were only introduced into Russia in the second half of the century. Peter was in debt to the West for many things, but not for money to finance his wars and capital construction.

In 1701 taxation brought in about twice as much as in 1682; in 1724, allowing for the results of Peter's constant depreciation of the currency, over three times as much as in 1682. But in the years 1703 to 1710, despite the ingenuity of Peter's "profit-seekers" (see p. 47), revenue not only failed to keep up with the mounting expenditure, but even declined. The burdens of conscription and forced labour were added to those of taxation. Arrears, evasion, and mass flights of peasantry were the regular rule.

Hitherto the greater part of the revenue had come from indirect taxation; now, as his finances stumbled from bad to worse, Peter turned to a reorganization of the main direct tax, that on households. It was levied on assessments made in 1678. To bring these up to date Peter ordered in 1710 a new census of households. The resultant figures showed "emptiness"; not an increase, but a large decrease. Evasion of the census takers was on a gigantic scale, partly owing to the complicity of many landowners. For eight years Peter toiled with revised figures and numerous projects presented to him by Russian and foreign reformers for revision of taxation, increase of commerce and production, and improvement of the lot of the peasantry.

Meanwhile the same tale continued of grim financial struggle in all quarters. In the end Peter decided to levy a poll-tax and out of the proceeds meet the requirements of the army. In this decision he was much influenced by French example and his first steps towards a poll-tax were taken at the time of his visit to France, but certain of the projects put forward earlier by Russian reformers included this suggestion.

A poll-tax required another census. In 1718 orders were issued to inscribe all males in all classes of the peasantry and in most classes in the towns. The resultant census was the most terrible of all Peter's inquisitions. It took years to complete, and in the end the army had to be used on a ferocious scale to enforce registration. For "concealment" he decreed the death penalty. The new tax was levied for the first time in 1724 on 5,569,000 "souls," of whom only 169,000 were townsfolk. Despite large, immediate arrears, it at once provided over half the total revenue. It was intended, not as a war measure, but as a permanent tax for the upkeep of the army. The cost of the army was estimated and then the amount of the tax fixed so as to bring in the sum required. Peter meant the poll-tax to last, and it did. It remained the largest item in the revenue until the end of the century, and though it subsequently declined in relative importance, it was not abolished until 1886.

A "soul" was the treasury poll-tax paying unit, every male irrespective of age and condition in every village, commune, or town inscribed in the census return. Following Peter's census, "revisions" were taken every twenty or twenty-five years, but between each such interval the poll-tax was assessed on the number of "souls" recorded in the previous census. The actual apportionment of the tax to individuals was left, as was customary in Muscovite practice, to each commune or local community. This had a double effect. It increased the importance of the village commune, which in most parts of Russia was the organized body of the working peasantry, and it encouraged the growth of the custom of periodical redistribution of the peasants' strips in their common fields. Secondly, since the tax was a fixed amount per head without regard to the amount of land a peasant worked or the amount of money he earned, it led to an extension of arable land. Further, as regards the landowners' serfs, the landowners themselves were soon made responsible for the collection of the poll-tax from their serfs. Thus, they became even more closely linked up with the government as the indispensable police-tax supervisors of the peasantry.

While the effect of Peter's actions and legislation did much to shape the social structure of the peasantry and the landowners, it did very little to raise the low productivity of Russian agriculture. In contrast with his continuous and decisive impulsion of industry, mining, and commerce, his efforts to improve agriculture were intermittent, sporadic, and ineffectual. It is insignificant that he created a commerce college, a mines college, and a manufactures college, but no agriculture college. Something was done to extend the cultivation of hemp, flax, and tobacco, and to improve sheep-breeding and wool carding and combing. A few agricultural experts, or so-called experts, were hired from the Baltic provinces, Silesia, and Holland. Efforts were made to introduce Russian peasants to the advantages of harvesting with scythes instead of sickles (though oddly enough Peter did not think at the same time of making scythes in Russia). There was little enough success; as he himself wrote in his instructions on scythes: "you know yourselves that anything that is new, even though it is good and needful, will not be done by our folk without compulsion."

The same emphasis on compulsion recurs again and again in Peter's industrial and commercial policy, but here he was able to accomplish much in various fields, despite the crudity of many of his measures. Much that is typical of his outlook is exemplified in the following decree that he issued in 1723: "Either our decrees are not accurately observed, or there are few people who wish to go into the business of manufacturing. Manufactures too are ruined by goods brought from abroad. For instance, a peasant discovered a dye called "Florence lake." I had artists try it. They said it was inferior only to the Venetian, and quite equal to the German; some said even better. A good deal of it was made, but no one buys it on account of the quantity bought from abroad. That there are few people wishing to go into business is true, for our people are like children, who never want to begin the alphabet unless they are compelled by their teacher. It seems very hard to them at first, but when they have learnt it they are thankful. So in manufacturing affairs we must not be satisfied with the proposition only, but we must act and even compel, and help by teaching, by machines, and other aids, and even by compulsion, to become good economists. For instance, where there is fine felt we should compel people to make hats, by not allowing the sale of felt unless a certain number of hats are made."

The economic policy of Peter is usually described as mercantilist—an epithet of mystifying vagueness. It is true that he looked upon wealth as a means of state power, and set great store on the acquisition of bullion, on a high import tariff, and on state regulation of trade, all four of which features were in varying degrees common to most western European doctrine and practice of the time. But neither Peter nor his advisers studied western theory deeply or methodically imitated the systematic application of Colbert or the Great Elector. As always, he worked by jolts empirically, trying this and that method or device, ordering and counter-ordering, untied by economic dogma, prepared to use any means to surmount an obstacle or launch a new venture.

The net result of twenty-five years of hectoring impulsion was that Peter bequeathed a large-scale new heavy industry and a greatly developed textile industry, introduced several new branches of manufactures, and wrenched foreign trade round from Archangel to St. Petersburg. Foreign seaborne trade by the end of his reign was quadrupled in value. In order to foster the growth of commerce through St. Petersburg, he almost killed Archangel. It was not even the second port in the empire: Riga far outdistanced it. Both in shipping and in the handling of foreign commerce the English and the Dutch retained their virtual monopoly, and this was of greatly enhanced importance now that Peter had so largely increased the export of naval stores, thanks to his Baltic conquests.

As usual, it was the needs of war that originally concentrated Peter's energies on developing Russian industry. Guns, ships, all sorts of munitions, sailcloth, and woollen cloth for uniforms had the priorities. In Muscovy industry was for the most part scattered in small-scale handicraft workshops, which met the demand for consumers' goods. These continued to function much as before, though every now and then Peter would attempt to improve their quality or regulate their products by launching impossible orders —for instance, for a better method of curing leather or for a wider linen weave. In addition to this domestic industry, Peter inherited the beginnings of a relatively concentrated large-scale metal industry, which mainly worked for the military requirements of the state.

From this slender basis he built up a heavy industry, which in the end supplied all the ordnance requirements both of his army and of his navy; a rope, sail, and lumber industry which met all the needs of his navy, and a cloth industry which furnished uniforms for a large proportion of his troops. He hoped that his stimulation of cloth manufacture would enable him to dispense entirely with imports, but, in fact, he still had to have recourse to Yorkshire woollens, or to their Prussian and Silesian rivals, though in greatly reduced quantities.

Peter was a man who delighted in the blessings bestowed upon Joseph, the chief things of the ancient mountains and the precious things of the lasting hills. He never tired of seeking out rare specimens of minerals or stones. Every inducement was given both "to our faithful subjects" and to "all foreign volunteers . . . to devote single-minded love and inclination to mining works." To the old-established metal-working centres of Tula and Olonets he added those of the Urals, whose riches had hitherto hardly been touched.

In 1695, apart from numerous small forges, there were seventeen iron-works in Muscovy, none of them in the Urals. Between that date and 1725 fifty-two iron-works were started, of which thirteen were in the Urals. These last had far larger furnaces and were better equipped than most of those elsewhere. In his closing years Peter entrusted the Urals state iron- and copper-works to Henning, a thoroughly competent technician and organizer, who had been taken into Russian service when "the grand embassy" was in Holland, and ever since had done sterling work in artillery and mining work. Thanks to Henning, the Urals state iron-works by 1725 were producing about twenty per cent of the whole Russian production, while another twenty per cent was produced by the private iron-works in the Urals, concentrated in the hands of Demidov, Peter's chief mining-metallurgical entrepreneur, who founded a long-lasting line of iron barons. Of copper production the Urals had almost a complete monopoly.

This was one of Peter's lasting bequests. The Urals heavy industry, built up on the proximity of rich supplies of high-grade ore, abundant water power, and plentiful charcoal supplies, continued to prosper and expand throughout the eighteenth century, and it remained the most important centre of the iron industry until the rise of the south Russian region in the eighteen-sixties. Already by 1716 a little Russian iron of excellent quality was appearing on the London market. By the time of Peter's death, Russian production of pig-iron was probably slightly larger than the English output. Within twenty-five years it far outdistanced that of England, and by the time of Catherine the Great Russia had supplanted Sweden as the largest producer in Europe and the largest iron exporter to England.

Most of the new iron-works began by being owned and run by the state. This was a general feature of the Petrine industrial development. Between 1695 and 1709 nearly three-quarters of the new manufactories were state works, and nearly all of them were designed for military and naval needs. Between 1710 and 1725 the picture changes, as the needs of war become rather less absorbing. The new works in his later years were far less concentrated on military needs; silk, velvet, and ribbon manufactories were started; china, glass, and brick-works made their appearance. A number of the state factories were handed over to private operation, and Peter pressed forward the opening of new works by individuals or companies, granting them important exemptions and privileges. Similarly, the earlier policy of extension of state monopolies was abandoned later in favour of their drastic diminution.

Already in 1699 Peter began his persistent drive for the formation of companies, in imitation of western countries, to develop the resources of Russia and undertake manufacturing. A Dutchman commented at that time that Peter's initiative need not cause apprehension, since the Russians did not know how to start or carry on such companies. In the main he proved correct. Neither by driving nor luring could Peter succeed in laying solid foundations. Various companies were duly formed, some of the most notorious headed by the great men of the land, but they were very unstable and several of them were scandalously mismanaged. The companies were of varying types: some concentrated on trading, others operated mills or works. All were regulated, in the sense that the state kept close control over them, "as a mother over a child." It also granted them special privileges and exemptions, which aroused much opposition as giving them monopolistic advantages. Within a few years of Peter's death most of the then remaining companies ceased operation or passed into the hands of a single proprietor. Yet his policy of company promoting by the state was continued by his successors, and was not abandoned until the time of Catherine the Great.

Peter succeeded to a large extent in his efforts to find capital for industrial development from the merchant-traders, though the state itself had to provide much assistance. He was far less successful in drawing off the capital of the landowners. They played but a small part at this time in manufacturing concerns. The largest share both in financing and in organizing and operating the private works fell to the small group of big-scale merchant-traders, who were already before Peter's day closely linked with the government and were indispensable in finance.

Although foreign industrial entrepreneurs played a fairly prominent rôle and foreign specialists a very important one, foreign capital played no part. No instance is known of any establishment started during Peter's reign from imported capital. The foreign element is sometimes exaggerated, and it should be realized that some of the best-known foreigners were more or less thoroughly Russianized, having been already at work in Russia before Peter grew up, or (like James Bruce) having been born and bred in Russia.

In technical capacities, however, as opposed to business and industrial organization, foreigners were of far greater importance, above all in shipbuilding. Peter's own personal devotion to tools, mechanical devices, and inventions acted as a powerful spur to the continued recruiting of foreign technicians to teach the Russians new processes. In reverse, there was a similar, but smaller, flow of Russian artisans and merchants sent abroad to pick the brains of westerners. The results were of consequence in the new industries and to a certain extent in the heavy industry, but the great majority of Russian operatives were weavers, spinners, smiths, potters, etc., working in small-scale shops or at home on the "put-out" system, and these in the main remained unaffected by the changes introduced through Peter.

The greatest difficulty lay in the recruitment of labour for the new plants, particularly in St. Petersburg and the Urals, which had very little local labour to draw upon.

For so rapid an expansion the shortage of skilled artisans was acute. The new technical schools and strict regulations on apprenticeship provided some remedy, but only a slight one. To the end Peter was calling for more and more trained artificers, and having to make do with learners or all-round handy men.

There has been much discussion recently among Soviet historians as to whether the bulk of the men recruited for the mines and industries were hired workers or ascribed serfs and other types of compulsory labour. The answer is not as yet final, but it seems clear that the state works, especially the Ural mines, depended to a large extent for unskilled and semi-skilled labour on ascribed state peasants, while in the private works hired workers played a larger part. The motley labour force for the very rapid industrial expansion was drawn in the main from the townsfolk and the state peasants, but all and sundry, including criminals and vagrants, contributed a quota. The landowners did what they could to prevent the attachment to works of their runaway serfs, and, since very few of them were as yet concerned in manufacturing, their interests clashed persistently with those of the merchant-industrialists.

These latter found hands so difficult to obtain and keep that Peter granted them special privileges, and in 1721 he went so far as to place them almost on an equality with the landowners by allowing them to buy serfs for permanent attachment to mines or factories. This right, which created a new class of serfs called professional serfs, was in fact little used during his few remaining years, but later the number of such serfs rapidly increased. As a consequence, the right became a bitter bone of contention with the landowning class which considered its hitherto exclusive privilege of owning serfs dangerously compromised, and sought, ultimately with success, to maintain intact its monopoly rights.

The industrial development so harshly fostered by Peter was in many respects new. The location map of industry was fundamentally changed by the appearance on it of St. Petersburg and the Urals. New types of goods were produced. The foundation of companies was new. Ascription of peasants to plants was new. The scale of many of the new works was very much larger than heretofore. Yet at the same time there was no sundering break with the past. Although a few works employed as many as seven hundred or even a thousand workers, the industrial unit was usually still a collection of scattered workshops, not one single factory. As in the past, it frequently had the characteristics of a colonial settlement rather than of a single establishment. The terrible conditions of labour, the wastage on many of the works started, their complete or very large dependence on the state were salient features of the economic history of Muscovy before Peter. The failure of his companies and craft guilds, his depreciation of the currency by nearly one-half, and his ultra-protectionist tariff of 1724, which was almost immediately abandoned after his death, have been counted heavily against him. The charge has been levelled that his development of manufacturers was a hothouse growth which withered away.

These and other strictures have a certain justification. Yet, taken all in all, Peter inspired the economic life of Russia with a new impetus. Mining and industrial development, though its rate of increase declined sharply after his death, leapt forward under Elizabeth and Catherine the Great. The main lines of this development were for the most part laid under Peter. He gave canals to Russia: the price was terrible, but he linked the Volga to the Baltic, and his successors followed in his wake. Russia's foreign trade quadrupled in value under Peter, with a large active balance in her favour. It grew apace throughout the eighteenth century, flowing mainly through his creation, St. Petersburg, and through his acquisition, Riga. The staple exports continued to be the same as in the seventeenth century, but they were greatly expanded; the one addition, iron, originated with Peter. He found Muscovy as an economic power undeveloped; he left Russia stronger and more developed, though for the time being overstrained.

Chapter 10

Peter the Great, Emperor of Russia

NOTHING IS MORE striking in the personality of Peter than his dominating will, unless it be his restless, inexhaustible activity of mind and body. "The All-Russian Emperor," as his title now ran, hardly ceased celebrating the peace of Nystad after twenty-one years' struggle in the West, before he turned to the East and regrouped part of his army in preparation for yet another war in the coming spring, war against Persia. Having won his way on the Baltic, without pause he plunged southwards to dominate the Caspian.

This was no sudden idea. Persia and the Caspian had for some six years past been much in his mind. For all the concentration of his main energies upon Europe, he had from his earliest years taken a lively interest in Asia. The enthusiasm of the explorer was allied with the gold-dazzled phantasy of the prospector and the merchant. Time and again he was harbouring schemes to tap the fabled wealth of Cathay, ever since as a youth he heard of a recent Muscovite mission to the Great Mogul, and drank in accounts of China and the rich trade to be tapped by caravans from Siberia.

In his boyhood China and Muscovy, with her far-flung Cossacks, were contending for the lands watered by the Amur. The contest ended to the advantage of the Chinese in 1689, when the first treaty of the Celestial Empire with any European state was signed, and the Amur region was kept by the Chinese for the next hundred and sixty years. The same treaty also provided for mutual commercial relations, which had recently begun but only on a precarious and restricted basis. Thereafter Russo-Chinese contacts increased much, primarily through the caravan trade in furs and silk, and it became Peter's persistent object to extend this trade and to establish a permanent mission in Pekin. He did his best to make effective the state monopoly in the very profitable fur trade with China, and he despatched two large missions to Pekin to negotiate better terms and regale his unquenchable thirst for information. They failed to secure his objects, but the way was marked out and in 1728 another treaty gave to Russia, at least on paper, what he had aimed at.

Peter never sought to challenge Chinese power, either on the Amur region or elsewhere. This was as well, for the Manchu dynasty was at its apogee under the great emperor Kiang-hi (1662–1722), and was engaged in reconquering Mongolia from the Kalmuks. Peter in the main confined himself to commercial affairs, and refrained from over-adventurous leaguing with China's foes.

It was only to the north on the inhospitable Pacific that he moved forward the Far Eastern boundaries of Russia by his conquest of Kamchatka and annexation of the Kurile islands. Fired like Elizabethan mariners with the lure of a north-east passage, he determined to solve the debated problem whether Asia and America were joined together, and at long last, almost on his death-bed, he sent out Behring on the first of his Arctic expeditions to the straits that bear his name. Sixty years later Russian posts were dotting the Alaskan seaboard; ninety years later one such was founded only a few miles north of San Francisco.

A year before despatching Behring, Peter sent off two frigates under sealed orders in the opposite direction "to the illustrious King and Owner of the glorious island of Madagascar" (1723). The real purpose of this ill-equipped expedition was to go on to India and conclude a commercial treaty with the Great Mogul. Incidentally it was to bring back some teak on which he could practise his skill. Thirty years earlier he had sent a merchant envoy to the court of Aurungzbe. To the end Peter sought routes to India and means of tapping its reputed wealth; and to the end he never forgot his carpenter's bench.

The Madagascar project proved a fiasco. One of the ships sprung a leak while still in the Baltic, and both returned incontinently to Reval. Peter was furious at this failure; but the sea route to India was only a casual diversion; for many years past his attention had been fastened on the land routes through Central Asia and Persia, where the silk trade had long been a magnet for Muscovy, as for England and the Netherlands.

In Central Asia the two rival oasis khanates of Khiva and Bokhara were ancient centres of Moslem culture and caravan trade. They were separated from the Muscovite empire by the immense steppe lands of the nomad Turkoman, Kazakh, and Kalmuk hordes between the Caspian, the River Ural, and the borders of China. Hitherto Muscovite connections had been limited to Cossack-nomad clashes and intermittent caravans to and from Samarkand and Khiva. In Peter's day Central Asia once again was in movement. The Kalmuks, then the strongest power in the steppes, being pressed hard by the Chinese, were in turn pressing hard upon the Kazakhs, as well as upon Bokhara, which after a period of great renown fell into disunity (1702) and was in continued enmity with Khiva.

Under Peter, Russia was active on every frontier. In 1700 and 1703 he received embassies from the khan of Khiva appealing for protection from Bokhara. He was too engrossed in war with Sweden to take any practical action, but eleven years later when another appeal came from the khan his hands were less tied. He was at that same time drinking in tales from a Turkoman adventurer of river gold in the Central Asian sands, of the old course of the Oxus flowing into the Caspian instead of the Aral Sea, and of the routes to India. Thereupon (1714) Peter decided to mount a large expedition to explore, trade, and seek gold; to bring Khiva, and Bokhara if it proved possible, into subjection, and to send forward a detachment up the Oxus and on to India. The expedition, 3,500 strong, explored the eastern Caspian, and then struck across the desert for Khiva (1716–17). There it found a new, unfriendly khan. After beating his troops, it ignominiously fell into the simplest of traps and was butchered almost to the last man.

This signal disaster coincided with Russian thrusts from the side of Siberia, whence Peter sent out four expeditions into the Central Asian steppes (1714–22). The quest for gold, which was uppermost, proved fruitless, but the confines of Siberia were successfully advanced; Omsk was founded (1717); with the Kazakhs closer relations were knit, which twenty years later were to have important consequences. Russian knowledge of these steppe regions was greatly extended, and the first history and geography of the Kalmuk lands was written. Siberia under Peter became not only a land of convict labour (and of Swedish prisoners of war), but also a land with growing agriculture and with the first beginnings of mining. It was ceasing to be dominated by the fur interest, but it did not become what he hoped it would, a land of gold, until the nineteenth century.

The Khivan expedition coincided also with further activity on the Caspian and in Persia. In 1715 Peter appointed one of his most energetic "fledglings," Volynsky, to undertake a mission to the shah. His instructions, revised by Peter's own hand, included a commercial treaty and full information on the condition, resources, and communications of Persia, especially those with India, as well as on the silk trade and the possibility of killing the overland route through Turkey by diverting the whole trade to Russia. Special attention was to be given to the Armenians. Volynsky concluded a commercial treaty (1717), which gave Russian merchants valuable openings, but the most important consequences of his mission were that it revealed to Peter the extreme weakness into which Persia had sunk and created additional links with the Georgians and Armenians in Transcaucasia. Further reconnaissances were made to chart the Caspian and spy out routes. Volynsky was made governor of Astrakhan, whence he continued to prepare the ground and sent Peter reports urging that with but a small army the Persian silk provinces along the Caspian could be seized.

In December 1721 Peter received the news of outrages committed on Russian merchants in Transcaucasia by the wild Lesghian mountaineers of Daghestan, nominal subjects of the shah. "Now is the very occasion for which you were ordered to prepare"; so Peter wrote to Volynsky. Immediately news followed that the shah had been deposed by an Afghan revolt. The Safavi dynasty was at the last stage of collapse and Persia in the throes of anarchy. Peter launched out on his Caspian venture.

He found Transcaucasia divided between Persia and the advancing Ottoman empire. To the north of the Caucasus along the Terek river, flowing into the Caspian, ran the shadowy southern limits of his own empire, the rough, frontier land of the Terek Cossacks. For the last century and a half Muscovite connections had been slowly increasing with the peoples of the Caucasus, and with the two ancient Christian peoples, the Georgians and the Armenians, living beyond the mighty range.

Armenian merchants played a great rôle in the silk trade, so much coveted by Peter, and were regular go-betweens with Muscovy through Astrakhan. The various Georgian principalities were divided amongst themselves in internecine rivalry. Many of their nobility were much Persianized and often found it convenient to embrace Islam. Yet they also found it convenient to look northwards to the Orthodox tsar, far away though he was in Moscow.

Alexis had specially close relations with Georgian rulers, and one of them took refuge for a time in Muscovy and had his grandson brought up there. During the regency of Sophia another refugee Georgian prince ensconced himself under Muscovite protection, and Peter befriended his son and entered him in his guards, one of the first of a long line of Georgian noblemen to distinguish themselves highly in the Russian army. Various ecclesiastics, among them an exceptionally persistent and ingenious Armenian, added their share to the increasingly close mutual relations.

Thus in the Transcaucasian Christians Peter had a complement to the Balkan Christians. He used their information for what it was worth, and had hopes of eventual material support, but he was not led astray by the high-flowing protestations that were the stock-in-trade of Caucasian anglers for money and support. Nor for his part did he issue any deluding proclamation calling on the Christians to rise, as he had done eleven years before in the Balkans. On the eve of his Persian campaign he instructed

Volynsky: "As to what you write about the prince of Georgia, give encouragement to him and the other Christians, if any of them are willing for this affair, but do not begin anything until the arrival of our troops, on account of the habitual recklessness of these peoples. . . ."

Unlike the earlier Romanovs, Peter was less interested in Georgia than in the coastal Caspian provinces of Persia. These were the main object of the war that he began in 1722. Nominally it was to aid the helpless shah to restore order in his own dominions. Actually it was to forestall the Turks and establish Russian control of the western and southern shores of the Caspian and thereby capture the silk trade.

Peter led his army in person, accompanied by Catherine. He sailed down the Volga to Astrakhan, where he had mustered a force of 30,000 troops and 5,000 sailors, in addition to large numbers of Cossacks and other irregular cavalry. Thence he sailed across to the Terek region with his infantry, while the cavalry went round by land, facing "indescribable labour in their march on account of lack of water and bad grass." Meeting with little organized resistance, he occupied without difficulty his first main objective, Derbent, an important strategical and trading centre on the coast. Thence he planned to seize Baku and send up a force to Tiflis to clinch the adherence of the strongest of the Georgian princes and of certain groups of Armenian mountaineers.

Both were in sizable strength and professed to be ready for action, once Russian support arrived on the scene. But the Georgian had to admit being challenged by a rival prince, and he could make no impression on the Lesghian confederacy in Daghestan. Peter did not repeat the gamble of thrusting forward in expectation of a Christian rising. It was late summer, and sickness took a terrible toll of his troops and horses. His supply fleet suffered severely in a storm. The Daghestan mountaineers were in dangerous force on his flank. He decided to withdraw to the Terek and Astrakhan. Once again Peter had showed himself far too over-confident and had trusted too much to uncompleted or extemporized plans. But he had no intention of abandoning his Caspian venture, and in those regions, with the star of the Persians at its lowest, a daring policy might reap a rich harvest.

In that same autumn (1722) a small detachment was sent to seize the Persian port of Resht, and in the next year Baku was occupied by larger forces. Simultaneously, a treaty was signed with the now derelict shah by which Peter undertook to defend him against his foes in return for the cession of the Persian seaboard provinces, already occupied at key-points by his troops.

At the same time the Turks entered upon the scene to vie with the Russians in annexations. They soon came to the edge of war with Peter. He was determined to block their path to the Caspian and to keep his hold there, but he continued to be cautious in his dealings with the Armenians and Georgians inland, whom the Turks were equally determined to keep from Russian clutches. After much entangled diplomatic wrestling a troubled agreement was reached (1724): Peter kept his coastal strip, and the Turks kept Georgia, which they had overrun, and suzerainty over their Sunni brethren in the fastnesses of Daghestan.

From his Persian expedition Peter returned, after two bouts of sickness, to Moscow in December 1722. There over the New Year and Twelfth Night revels he repeated the previous year's riot of grotesque masquerades, as of old with the "Prince Cæsar" and the "Prince Pope" and his "college of cardinals"; with Catherine appearing (in rôles very suitable to her style of beauty) now as a Frisian peasant woman, now as an amazon accompanied by all her court as negroes or as sailors; with Peter himself dressed as a naval captain in command of a two-decked frigate under full sail mounted on sledges. From wild revelling he plunged as usual with equal energy into affairs of state, struggling with yet another overhaul against rapaciousness and injustice. Even the topmost poppies fell or were bent low. Nesterov, the chief "fiscal," was executed; Shafirov was disgraced; Menshikov passed under a dark cloud and had to disgorge more of his vast acquisitions.

Although nearly all the foreign diplomats depicted the

internal condition of Russia and her future in the darkest colours, and although the new emperor was recognized as such only by Prussia, Sweden, and the Netherlands, there was everywhere lively recognition of his power and much apprehension of his capacity for startling action. Nowhere was this more so than in the Baltic.

Internal divisions in Sweden gave Peter every opportunity to establish his influence at Stockholm. Both George I and Frederick IV of Denmark feared the worst from the far-reaching designs they attributed to him in Holstein and Mecklenburg, and Frederick was also faced with demands for Russian exemption from the Sound dues. Their alarms were further increased when early in 1724 Russian influence in Stockholm rose so high that a defensive alliance was made between the two ex-enemies, which included an ominous provision for joint action to obtain satisfaction for the duke of Holstein. A British diplomat belittled such an alliance as being "like Daniel's dream, a toe of clay to an image of brass, which can never consolidate." In the long run he was right, but for the time being the newcomer in the Baltic had preponderant power.

Soon after concluding this alliance, Peter decided on the marriage, long bruited, of his eldest daughter Anna with the duke of Holstein, and in December 1724 their official betrothal took place. Thus Russia definitely espoused the cause of Holstein, which was to be for many years to come in the forefront at St. Petersburg. Anna, a tall, handsome brunette, who won universal admiration for her intelligence, manners, and spirit, was a first-rate advertisement for her father's insistence on western education. Her betrothed, the duke, had a warm friend in Catherine, but Peter himself had little personal regard for him—it was three years before he even invited him to a private dinner—and for long he had hankered for a far more illustrious match, a marriage into the Bourbon house of France.

The failure of the 1717 treaty with France to bring the results that Peter hoped did not deter him from continuous attempts to refashion an effective alliance. Immediately after the treaty of Nystad he initiated proposals in Paris to this end, coupling them with the project of a marriage for Anna or Elizabeth, his second daughter. He hoped to use France as an offset to Great Britain and the Empire, but Dubois was a master of temporizing prolixity, and in the end there was no alliance and no marriage. Peter did, however, gain much-needed assistance from the French at Constantinople in his protracted and dangerous struggle with the Turks over Persia and the Caucasus.

The long-continued negotiations for a marriage of Anna or Elizabeth with the duke of Chartres were coupled with the project of the duke's election as king of Poland when Augustus II should die. This was thought likely to occur in the near future, which well it might have considering his manner of life, though in fact he lived on until 1733. The design against Augustus, one of whose great ambitions was to make his Polish crown hereditary, marks the length to which Peter had travelled in opposition to his erstwhile ally, and the closing years of his reign brought to the fore two new features in Peter's Polish policy, alliance with Prussia and energetic support of the Orthodox in Poland. Both features were to remain guiding-lines in Russian policy towards Poland throughout the rest of the century.

In 1720 Peter concluded a treaty with Frederick William, the first of a long series of similar treaties with Prussia and Austria culminating in the first partition of Poland (1772). Thereby the free, elective constitution of the Polish monarchy and the "liberties" of Poland, including the famous *liberum veto*, were to be preserved intact. This was the riposte of Peter to the lining up of Augustus II with the emperor and George I (*cf.*, p. 105). The treaty meant, in effect, a Russo-Prussian combination to keep Poland weak, distracted, and unreformed. It did not, however, mean a Russian intention to partition Poland.

Schemes of partition had been broached already in the seventeenth century, though not by Muscovy, and were repeatedly put forward by Frederick William and by Augustus himself. They involved the lopping off of portions of Poland, then the second largest country in Europe, but by no means the disappearance of Poland as a state. Peter neither proposed nor planned any considerable diminution of Poland, save as regards the vassal fief of Courland, which he succeeded in keeping as a Russian pawn. He preferred to hold fast to what had become his policy of checkmating Augustus's designs and of maintaining Russian influence in Poland by bribery, intimidation, and force, playing off against each other Augustus and the confederation of his Polish opponents. It was aptly said at the time: "He has built his system upon the dissensions of this country and with the design of making them arise should they not appear of themselves."

There was little need to foster dissensions. The weakness of Poland and her internal strife were aggravated, but not originated, by Russia or any other power. This was true even of the vexed question of the Dissidents, the Orthodox, and Protestant minorities in the heterogeneous Polish lands. Russian claims in support of the large Orthodox minority in eastern Poland dated back to Peter's boyhood, when it was laid down in the Russo-Polish treaty of 1686 that the Orthodox were not to be oppressed in any way by the Catholics or Uniates. No energetic action was taken to make a reality of this article until 1718.

From that time onwards Peter intervened on behalf of the Orthodox more and more strongly. He installed in Poland a special commissary to deal with the numerous incidents and disputes between Orthodox, Catholic, and Uniate, and he worked hard to try to secure that the religious and civil liberties of the Orthodox were written into the constitution. When in 1724 there was a "massacre" of Protestants by Catholics at Thorn, which aroused international concern, Peter took the lead in denouncing the Polish Catholics and demanding the most extreme penalties. Thus he placed in the forefront of Russo-Polish relations the question of the Dissidents, which was to be so fruitful a weapon in the hands of his successors. It was the Polish, not the Balkan, Orthodox who were the first to receive effective aid from the heavy hand of Russia.

In 1724 Peter was but fifty-two, but he was suffering from strangury and stone, and his bouts of illness were now much more frequent and serious. His gusty fits of choler had grown with the years; then he was fatal when his eyes rolled so, and only his wife could assuage those terrifying convulsions. Now more than ever the path to imperial favours lay through Catherine, crowned as empress in the spring of 1724. Yet even she fell under her husband's disfavour. Late in that same year her chamberlain and close confidant, William Mons, brother of Peter's early mistress, was convicted of gross and long-continued peculation and jobbery. Great publicity was given to the scandalous affair, which rumour bedaubed with smirching of the empress herself. Mons was sentenced to execution. Catherine was confident that she could persuade Peter to pardon him. She failed.

The execution of Mons was the last great stroke delivered by Peter in the battle against malpractices and corruption, which he was waging with deadly vigour during his last two years. A special commission was appointed to aid him. Its head asked: "Shall I cut out the knots only, or lay the axe to the roots?" "Fell to the ground," was the reply.

"We are on the eve of some sad extremity," wrote one; "the misery increases from day to day." The harvests of 1722 and 1723 were very bad. The continuing operations in Persia sucked up more and more money. "Discontent . . . in all ranks," a foreign observer summed up, "could not well be greater than now. But as a chief is lacking, and as in this humbled nation, so accustomed to slavery, fear is great, I cannot believe that in this emperor's lifetime anything can break out, although this government is very similar to that of tsar Ivan the Terrible." All trembled before the "despotic power which allows no one to possess anything which he can call his own."

The murky tension of these closing years was intensified by doubt as to the succession. Left undecided by the emperor (see pp. 99–100), it was clouding every issue, nourishing cankerworms, dividing his ministers into scheming cabals. That generation in Britain knew full well, as none other has ever since, the evils that uncertainty of succession to the throne begets in politics and government alike. These evils were nothing new to Muscovy. Peter as a youth had suffered them dangerously enough. He did not escape them in his prime or now nearing his end. Russia was haunted by them for a whole century to come.

At times Peter was gay and confident that his labours were bearing good fruit and that his heritage was secure. Few shared such optimism. St. Petersburg was almost as unpopular as ever. The labour gangs still toiled there, as on the Ladoga canal: "This is, as it were, the bottomless pit in which innumerable Russian subjects perish and are destroyed." The upper class cursed as ever the expense of having to build houses and live in a remote marsh, far from supplies and their regular haunts.

None the less, St. Petersburg was growing fast, and its position as a great port assured. Ten years earlier one foreign diplomat compared it to "a heap of villages linked together, like some plantation in the West Indies." Later he styled it "a wonder of the world, considering its magnificent palaces . . . and the short time that was employed in building it." In actual fact, it was very far from being as yet the majestic capital that Rastrelli and others created in the second half of the century.[1] Peter had no taste for sumptuous buildings, and was economical, even parsimonious, in his personal expenditure and his own court, though he allowed his wife ample scope and required of his grandees lavish hospitality.

The capital was graced now, if boorishly in western eyes, by Peter's new "assemblies"; mixed evening parties, two or three times a week, with dancing, cards, chess, and forfeits. These he had instituted immediately after returning from Paris in 1717. The hosts were designated by Peter himself, and he required that the guests should be drawn from a wide variety of persons and not confined to the aristocracy. Unlike most of his entertainments, there was no heavy drinking at the "assemblies," and they were a genuine and successful essay in accustoming Russian society to the novelty of social intercourse between men and women on a more or less western model.

[1] See the description of St. Petersburg in G. Scott Thomson, *Catherine the Great and the Expansion of Russia* (a volume in this series).

Peter spent the last year of his life in St. Petersburg and thereabouts. His health grew steadily worse, and at times he would withdraw in unaccustomed, morose aloofness. Despite his doctors, he was frequently on the move—to visit his new residence at Peterhof near by, with its fountains which he prized so highly (now utterly ruined by the Germans); to inspect salt works near Novgorod and the Ladoga canal, new factories and neighbouring shipyards; to take the Olonets waters and there enjoy himself hammering out sheets of iron. He was constantly cruising, constantly carousing, rather less constantly at work. A few weeks before his death he was not only taking the final decisions for the creation of his long-meditated Academy of Sciences, but was also revising details of the bacchanalian rites that he had instituted thirty years before and never abandoned.

Always he had lived at full stretch; he had grown to great stature as a statesman, warrior, and ruler, but in his grosser man he remained as he was as a youth. One of his doctors, a Scotsman, high in eulogy of "the unbounded genius of this great and active prince," declared that his "failings . . . principally, if not solely, arose from his inclination to the fair sex." Another admirer, at second hand, appositely summed up: "In short, for a king he was as little elegant as expensive in his amours: as in things of the highest moment, so in this he acted according to his inclinations without any regard to forms."

In mid-November 1724, when he was sailing off to visit some iron-works, a boat was shipwrecked before his eyes. He leapt into the icy water and laboured indefatigably at rescue work. He was inflamed with a fever, and though he was soon intermittently hustling about again, he was a stricken man. The strangury and stone returned. At the end of January 1725 he was in great pain and unable to leave his bed. In the early morning of February 8, unconscious for the last thirty-six hours, he died.

The death of Peter was acclaimed abroad with jubilation everywhere, save in Berlin where Frederick William alone of sovereigns ordered court mourning "for his dearest friend." No longer would the "northern Turk" disrupt the balance of Europe; now his surcharged country would relapse into internal broils and impotence. No one indeed could fill the place of so wholly an exceptional ruler as Peter, and decline there was bound to be; but there was no such breakdown as many expected. Catherine was immediately proclaimed empress without opposition, thanks to swift last-minute decisions by Menshikov and other adherents, and to the devotion of the guards to their dead emperor and his consort.

At once the official pæans began. Peter was lauded as "a Joseph who hath enlarged thy stores, and enrich'd thee with all good things, such as thou never before enjoyd'st! A Joseph, who hath brought thee out of darkness into light, out of ignorance into knowledge, out of contempt into glory . . .!" So Russia was told in funeral sermons, and for long afterwards in orations, odes, and anniversary outpourings. It is true that much genuine pride was felt in the new position in the world that Russia now occupied, thanks to Peter, but most of his subjects were far more conscious of the price they had to pay for "glory." Nothing is more revealing than a vivid, popular woodcut issued at this time and widely circulated for long afterwards which bore the title "The mice bury the cat."

What was the legacy of Peter? How much of it survived? What is his place in history?

First and most obviously, he transformed Russia's foreign relations. For a century before Peter, Muscovy had been tentatively and spasmodically linking herself closer with the West. Now henceforward Russia played her part as one of the main participants in European history. One dry, prosaic fact speaks for much: on Peter's accession he found his country with only one regular mission abroad, in Warsaw; on his death he left his representatives accredited to almost all the courts of Europe. For long Russia's part was confined to diplomacy, politics, and war. Within ten years of Peter's death she decided the issue of the Polish succession; within forty years the issue of the Seven Years' War in Europe; within ninety years the issue of Napoleon. Later her contribution was enlarged to cover the arts and sciences; and in this century it has been transformed by the Soviet revolution into one of the greatest world influences of our day.

Peter left no will (*cf.*, p. 100), and his so-called testament is a much-exaggerated, and in part fantastic, diatribe against Russian foreign policy in the eighteenth century. It was concocted originally by Napoleon's propagandists for the campaign of 1812, probably on the basis of a somewhat earlier analysis made by an *émigré* Pole. On the other hand, it is true that Peter initiated policies towards Poland, Sweden, and Turkey which his successors systematically developed.

For the first time in her history Russia was now indisputably stronger than her old enemy Poland. It was Peter's aim to use that strength so as to keep Poland internally weak, divided, and subject to dominant Russian influence, and to make of Courland a Russian preserve. This policy was continued after him with success, together with his practice of marching Russian troops at will through Polish territory for action in Germany. Later, Catherine the Great was led on to the policy of partition (1772, 1793) and finally to the total dismemberment of Poland by the three eastern powers (1795); a crime and a tragedy which has made the Polish question ever since one of the most intricate and intractable of European problems.

It was likewise Peter's policy after Nystad to keep Sweden internally weak, to encourage supporters of the Holstein line of succession, and to prevent any other foreign influences gaining ascendancy in Stockholm. As in Poland, Russian designs aimed at the maintenance of the oligarchical constitution in Sweden as the surest safeguard against a revival of her power. This policy his sucessors were able to continue for nearly fifty years, though with varying success, thanks to the divisions between the Caps and the Hats, to heavy subsidies and on one occasion to armed intervention. Twice Sweden struck back at Russia, vainly hoping to recoup herself for her losses in the Great Northern War (1741–3, 1788–90). By the end of the century, when the power of the monarchy in Sweden had been restored, Russians were considering the possession of Finland to be essential for the security of St. Petersburg (*cf.* p. 108), and Alexander I not only conquered Finland but, unlike Peter, retained it (1808–9).

At Stockholm, Peter's successors had to counter French diplomacy working steadily against them. The same was true at Warsaw and Constantinople. In his earlier years Peter had found the old French combination with Sweden, Poland, and Turkey directed against him. In his last years his efforts at close understanding with France achieved only partial and temporary success. The continued efforts of the empress Catherine were fatally rebuffed by Louis XV's government, with the result that Russia turned to the Habsburg rivals of the Bourbons. Within eight years of Peter's death France was supporting in arms Charles XII's former protégé, Stanislas Lesczyński, for the vacant throne of Poland against the Russian candidate; within fifteen years she was stirring up Sweden to attack Russia, and was intervening to such effect in Constantinople that Russia came virtually empty-handed out of a successful war against Turkey.

Although Elizabeth, enthused with French predilections and a sentimental hankering for Louis XV, was assisted to the throne by the intrigues of the French ambassador (1741), little political advantage accrued to France. The long and fruitful sway of French culture that now began in Russia stands in striking contrast with the almost continuous opposition or coldness of the two countries on the political plane down to 1789, except during the Seven Years' War when they fought on the same side. The persistent French support of Turkey, Sweden, and Poland remained an insurmountable obstacle to good relations. The French Revolution and Napoleon gave deeper cause for hostility. Almost continuously until the closing decades of the nineteenth century what had become the bastion of autocracy and reaction stood opposed to the progenitor of revolution and socialism and the inspirer of nationality.

The struggle in the Baltic brought Peter to the edge of open war with George I. Peter himself did all he could to divide Great Britain and Hanover, and was prepared to offer much to British commercial interests, believing rightly that in the end these would gain the upper hand in

London. Great Britain was far and away the biggest customer of Russia, and the large excess of Russian exports to her over imports from her was an invaluable source of much-needed specie. The refusal of Great Britain to accept the advent of the newly risen power in the Baltic played into the hands of her Dutch and Prussian trade rivals, and proved ineffective in attaining her essential aim, the safeguarding of the supply of naval stores, now largely in Russian hands.

When both George I and Catherine died in 1727, policy was reversed and Peter's forecast proved correct. Russia and Great Britain drew together in close and very profitable economic relations. Those ties remained the central strand in their mutual relations until the close of the century, even though the two countries fought on different sides, though not against each other, in the Seven Years' War. Thereafter the American War of Independence, Catherine the Great's armed neutrality, and incipient British alarms at her threatening expansion against Turkey ushered in a new period that took shape in the nineteenth-century contest over "the sick man of Europe" and "the threat to India." Peter the Great's establishment of Russia on the Baltic produced no contests between the bear and the lion comparable to those engendered by Catherine the Great's establishment of Russia on the Black Sea. Constantinople and the Straits were to range them in opposition to each other to an extent that Copenhagen and the Sound never did.

The Baltic legacy of Peter included his innovation of German marriages for his family. The consequences proved very far-reaching, though largely unintended. The innovation became the regular rule for all succeeding rulers of the Romanov dynasty. Save for the empress Elizabeth, who never married, they all took foreign and with one exception German wives. From the accession of Catherine the Great (1762) onwards the dynasty was in blood Russian only by virtue of Catherine's husband, the emperor Peter III, being the son of Peter the Great's daughter Anna, who had married the duke of Holstein. The result was that the upbringing of the Romanovs and the character of the court came to be largely German, and further that dynastic and family considerations played a conspicuous part in Russian foreign relations.

Already under Peter, Holstein, Mecklenburg, and Courland caused endless difficulties. Once his controlling hand was removed, these German connections involved Russia in a further influx of German princelings, courtiers, and adventurers, who entered upon a rancorous struggle for power with each other and with the Russian aristocracy (the so-called "period of favourites," 1725–41). The reign of the empress Anna (1730–40) became a byword for the predominance of her Courland favourites, and led to a nationalist resurgence in favour of Peter's daughter Elizabeth as empress and to an anti-German revulsion which opened the flood-gates to the dominance of French cultural influences. Within a generation of his death, Peter was looked back upon as a Russian patriot and beneficent despot who saw to it that Russians were not sacrificed to foreigners.

Under Elizabeth it was professedly in the name of what her foreign minister called "the system of Peter the Great" that he abandoned what had been a corner-stone of Peter's Baltic-German policy, friendship with Prussia. The reason for this change lay in the decisive and alarming successes of Frederick the Great, who proceeded to rival the exploits of Peter the Great and, like him, to place his country in the centre of the European stage. Prussia was now held to be "by reason of her proximity and of her great and threatening strength the primary and chief danger to Russia." Thus Russia joined in alliance with Austria, and in conjunction with France to attempt the abasement of Prussia in the Seven Years' War (1756–62).

Of all the major powers of Europe, Austria was the most consistently antipathetic in the eyes of Peter the Great. From his time dates the two centuries long rivalry of Russia and Austria in the Balkans. Yet with him was also initiated the attempt at common action against the Ottoman empire. Peter began by alliance with the emperor Leopold against the sultan (1697), but the treaty was scarcely signed before Leopold's victories enabled him to make peace on his own. At the very end of Peter's reign signs could be seen of a rapprochement with Vienna. The final collapse of Russian hopes of a French marriage and the withdrawal of French support for Russia in Constantinople led the empress Catherine to reinsure against the Turks by alliance on very favourable terms with Austria (1726).

The alliance, in varying forms, lasted for the greater part of the century, with one long break after the Seven Years' War. Twice Russia and Austria fought side by side against Turkey (1737–9; 1787–91); once against Prussia (1756–62). While Maria Theresa bewailed Russian inaction in the War of the Austrian Succession and had only too good cause to complain of desertion in 1762, Russia had heavy counts against her ally in 1739 and 1791. The western commitments of the Habsburgs, and above all mutual suspicion and rivalry, prevented the alliance from ever being firmly cemented or from leading to a partition of the Balkans such as was sketched under the empress Anna and later by Catherine the Great.

Peter himself had no such definite aim, but by a curious paradox, while in his own lifetime he accomplished so little against Turkey (in striking contrast with the victorious achievements of Austria) and is chiefly remembered for his disaster on the Pruth, he nevertheless set his stamp on Russian policy towards Turkey by bequeathing new ideas and new claims which shaped it for the rest of the century and far into the nineteenth.

He was the first to initiate successful offensive action against the Crimea, to strike south against Azov, to build a fleet, and to demand access to the Black Sea and freedom of navigation. Anna followed in his footsteps (1735–9), in the end to little advantage; Catherine the Great did likewise (1767–74, 1787–91), with triumphant results. The southern steppes and the Crimea passed into her hands, and the Black Sea ceased to be a Turkish lake.

Peter was the first to strike direct for the Principalities and the Danube. In every single one of the seven following Russo-Turkish wars, right down to 1878, Russian armies did likewise. He was the first to summon the Balkan Christians to rise against their Turkish masters and join hands with their Orthodox liberators. His descendants renewed the summons in diverse forms on diverse occasions. He was the first to demand that the Orthodox, not the Catholics, have the custody of the Holy Places in Jerusalem, a claim with a long subsequent history which figured prominently among the antecedents of the Crimean War. He was the first to demand a guarantee of religious freedom for the Orthodox in the Ottoman empire, a claim which was in part realized by Catherine the Great and was to prove one of the main causes of the Crimean War.

It is only too apparent that the importance of this legacy of Peter is in inverse ratio to the actual gains that he was able in the end to hand on after his catastrophe on the Pruth. He succeeded only in repudiating tribute to the Crimea, in securing the right to diplomatic representation in Constantinople and to pilgrimages to Jerusalem, and in barring the Turks from the Caspian. This last result was the one permanent outcome of his Persian venture, which had such ramifying consequences for Russian foreign relations during the three closing years of his life.

The involved struggle in the very unhealthy Caspian provinces, which Peter wrenched from Persia in collapse, was extremely costly and highly unpopular in Russia. After his death other counsels gained the day in St. Petersburg, and within the next ten years Russia handed back to a revived Persia Baku and the other occupied regions and withdrew to her former frontier. None the less, Turkey was kept from the Caspian. Not until half a century later was Peter's Caucasian advance renewed, as a result of which Catherine the Great and Paul brought Georgia into the Russian empire (1801), and Alexander I conquered and this time permanently retained Derbent and Baku (1813).

In his southern policy Peter, with his intrepid vision and over-sanguine energy, sketched the outlines of a rough programme that would take generations to fill in; but he disregarded one vital factor, colonization. Unlike Austria, Russia was not effectively contiguous with Turkey; the two empires were still separated by the debatable Black Sea steppe lands, across which neither power could strike sustainedly. Impatient for the offensive, Peter did not follow his predecessors in pressing forward defence lines or attracting new farmer settlers to the frontier. He struck against Turkey with a leap as it were. He struck against Persia by sea. To a large extent the later successes of Russia against Turkey and in the Caucasus depended on the fact that under Anna and Elizabeth, Catherine the Great and Alexander I, new defence lines were formed and an active colonization policy was pursued. To the extent that the southern steppes gradually became more like a base and less like nomad grazing and hunting grounds, it became possible for Peter's projects to be attained or furthered.

Colonization of a kind Peter did promote (and with his usual ruthlessness), but it was forced labour for his southern fleet, for his northern fleet and the construction of St. Petersburg, or for the Ural mines. None of the burdens he laid upon Russia were more onerous or bewailed, unless it be his conscription levies. There seemed indeed to be no end to the prodigious strains of every kind imposed on all classes for thirty years on end, no end to the series of shocks administered by the glowering taskmaster with his Pontic urge and ever-compulsive will. That was the deepest count of his subjects against him, and almost the only one that was felt alike by all. Russia needed some easing of unremitting toil and unsparing pace. With Peter's death alleviation came and for most of the next thirty years Russia took breath, but his work, though warped or for the time being laid aside, was not in the main undone.

The fate of Peter's legacy depended primarily on the dominant landowning class, the serf-owners. They had their counts against him, and the old, aristocratic families were for the most part deeply opposed; yet even to these latter Peter gave high and responsible posts, and the essential basis of his rule could never cease to be the common bond of the maintenance of serfdom. The adoption of western ways deeply antagonized the masses, but far less generally the upper class, among whom a number even of Peter's opponents, none the less, favoured western literature and culture.

Further, the serf-owners were much divided among themselves. Some of the grievances of the magnates against Peter found little or no echo among the smaller landowners, the army officers, or the lesser officials in state service, who could find ample opportunity to mount Peter's ladder of service and had no desire for a diminution of autocratic power by a reconstitution of the old Muscovite council of magnates, such as was attempted in 1730 by an oligarchical clique of old, noble families. Hence it was that the main essentials of Peter's reorganized absolutist state, with one great exception, survived the struggle for power among court factions and the disputed successions to the throne that filled the political canvas of the dismal "period of favourites" (1725–41).

The exception was compulsory state service for the serf-owners. Already under the empress Catherine I there was mitigation: the army and navy were heavily reduced. In the following reigns the obligations to serve were progressively whittled away, until in 1762 Peter III issued an edict completely freeing the serf-owners from service. Thus within little more than a generation one of the most important and unpopular features of Peter the Great's rule was erased.

On the other hand, there was no lessening of the bonds of serfdom; on the contrary, Peter's extension of serfdom suited the serf-owners only too well, and thereafter their power over their serfs became almost untrammelled. At the same time, however, entry into the privileged class of serf-owners, which had been facilitated by Peter, was being made increasingly difficult. The Russian serf-owners were becoming more and more confined to a hereditary estate of the nobility, somewhat equivalent to that in central Europe and France, an estate which was reorganized as such by the imperial charter of 1785.

These victories of the serf-owners were not extended to the abolition of Peter's legacy of a standing army. At the time of his death it numbered 210,000, apart from Cos-

sacks and various irregulars. For some years it was diminished in numbers, and the worst features of Peter's
quartering of the army throughout the country were eradi-
cated. But his system of conscription levies was retained,
and it was not long before military service again weighed
all too heavily on the peasantry. In the army itself, however, there was a strong core of patriotic pride. Peter
prized his soldiers, and they in return prized him and his
heritage, as their songs bear testimony. He was the creator
of the redoubtable Russian military tradition, the founder
of Russia as a great power in arms. For the last two and a
half centuries the world has had all too good cause to
know the legendary endurance and peasant toughness of
the army that Peter first fashioned.

He was even more the founder of the Russian navy, for
Muscovy had possessed no fleet at all. His first attempt,
the Azov fleet, foundered utterly, after costing an immense
outlay in labour and money. It was reserved to Catherine
the Great to create Russia's Black Sea fleet; and this she
did after land campaigns and the acquisition of the Crimea
(1783), not by striving, as Peter did, to build up a fleet
for the subjugation of the Crimea in the landlocked,
harbourless sea of Azov.

On the Baltic, on the other hand, Peter not only in-
novated, but built securely. When he died, the Baltic fleet
establishment was sixteen to seventeen thousand strong,
and there were some twenty-five men-of-war fit for sea,
in addition to the galley fleet. The navy was soon left to
dwindle for some time, but despite the continued unpopularity of naval service there was in fact no question of
abandoning Peter's handiwork. Russia with her new Baltic
coastline could but match the habits and practice of other
states.

Nor was St. Petersburg abandoned as the new capital.
For a few years indeed (1728–32) the seat of government was moved back to Moscow, but the old aristocracy
failed to maintain this success of theirs. The empress
Anna, with her western tastes and her crowd of German
favourites, returned to the Neva. Elizabeth, as the daughter of Peter, naturally remained there, combining in a

curious amalgam glorification of her father with Russian nationalism and a passion for French millinery. Not until 1918 did Moscow once again become the capital, when the Bolsheviks feared a German swoop on Petrograd. Thus the Petersburg period in Russian history is coincident with the imperial period, and each owes its origin and name to the emperor Peter the Great.

The rivalry between the two cities always remained strong, and Moscow continued to represent for most Russians the historic, spiritual, and cultural treasure-house of their country. A Russian poet later in the eighteenth century said in adulation that Peter the Great gave Russia her body, Catherine the Great her soul. The saying might be adapted: the old capital remained the symbol of the soul of Russia, while the new capital represented her power, her government, and her westernization.

Peter made the new capital in order to reap the full benefits of direct connections with the West, unhampered by the sway of the past that was so shackling in Moscow. The political reasons for the change were fused with his personal dislike and fear of Moscow, dating back to his early nightmare experiences there, and with his personal obsession for the noise of many waters and the tall ships riding the sea.

It may be argued that Peter would have acted more wisely if he had founded St. Petersburg as a new port, but had left Moscow as the capital. His enemies contended that St. Petersburg was unnecessary on all counts; that Riga was as near to Moscow, was a better port, and could well have served by itself as the direct outlet to the West, if such there must be. Europe had seen the making of two new capitals, Madrid and Warsaw, during the century or so before Peter, but neither were new as towns and both were centrally situated, as was Moscow. St. Petersburg, on the contrary, was far removed in bleak isolation on the periphery of an immense land empire stretching on and on to the Caucasus and the Pacific. St. Petersburg looked in the opposite direction, seawards, towards the Baltic lands and western Europe, and it was this that gave the stamp not only to so much of the city itself and the court, but ultimately to so much of the imperial government.

In consequence, Peter's foundation from the first has been taken as the greatest symbol of his westernization. He has repeatedly been attacked for having disrupted the ancient, indigenous, Orthodox culture of Muscovy by introducing an artificial, upper-class westernization, which resulted in the separation of Russia into two worlds, a small, educated European world and the vast mass of the peasant people. Before Peter, it is asserted, Muscovy was a world apart from Europe, the great representative of Orthodox Christianity. Owing to Peter, it is asserted, Russia came into being; a hybrid, more and more dominated by foreign influences, which looked upon her as but an adjunct of Europe destined to pursue the same path, and which repudiated the old unique Muscovite civilization.

Such charges raise fundamental questions: What is the destiny of Russia? Does she belong to the West? To Byzantium? To the East? To nothing but herself? That is why the question of the place of Peter in Russian history has so often merged into that of the place of Russia in world history, and that is why Peter, even apart from his extraordinary personality, has gripped the interest of posterity as no other Russian sovereign.

Within the limits of a brief biography it is not possible to do more than suggest that Muscovy was not in all essentials different from Europe, and that Peter should not be held responsible for later developments which were not intended by him and were not an inevitable outgrowth from his legacy. It is his successors rather than Peter himself who should bear the brunt of the charges just formulated. He should be judged primarily in the setting of his own times, not with our eyes on the nineteenth and twentieth centuries.

His own attitude towards westernization was at one and the same time crude, little premeditated, and yet complex. Although he was resolved to break away from the Moscow that spelt for him insurgent opposition and superstitious reaction, he was in his own impetuously selective way proudly conscious of the historic past of Russia. Ivan the Terrible had battled in vain during twenty-six years (1558–83) against Poland and Sweden to gain secure access to the Baltic by the conquest of Livonia and Estonia. When after twenty-one years' struggle with Sweden, Peter won these provinces and made a triumphal entry into Moscow, the streets were decorated with the portraits of Ivan and himself; on the one was written "he began," on the other "he completed."

Peter was anxious to impress on his subjects the necessity for his actions and policy by linking them up with those of his predecesssors, and to this end he caused various accounts of the Great Northern War to be written. They were written primarily for propaganda purposes, but the longest of them is a serious, well-weighed account, much corrected by Peter himself. In his later years he turned with reawakened interest to the history of the earlier tsars, and it was one of his most devoted younger servants, Tatishchev, who was inspired by him to become the first of modern Russian historians. It is entirely consonant with what he would have wished that from the middle of the century onwards he was repeatedly lauded as a specifically Russian national hero.

When Peter visited Paris in 1717, the French found that "the whole of this court take offence at the name Muscovite and even of Muscovy." These had hitherto been the usual designations employed in the West; now Russia and the Russians must take their place. And so it soon came to pass. The change in name in the West is indicative of what Peter had done for his country, and of the new position that she now occupied in European politics. Russia had emerged in place of Muscovy. But the contrast must not be exaggerated. For Peter and his countrymen Russia was no new term. Among the titles that he inherited was that of "tsar of all Russia," and the patriarch had been "patriarch of all Russia and all northern countries." Peter never intended a complete break with the past: he began with no far-reaching plan; in the end he came to aim at renovating Muscovy; he never aimed at replacing Muscovy by something quite new called Russia. Throughout his life and work the old and the new jostle each other and interpenetrate.

Some time in his later years he is reported to have said: "We need Europe for a few decades; then we can turn our backs on her." He found his country relatively weak and poor. She must go to school for a time, not in order to become a copy of her schoolmasters, but in order to learn from them the means whereby she could become powerful and prosperous in her own national way. Like Japan after 1867, she must borrow technique and certain externals. The deeper problems of cultural influence were in the main outside his range of vision. Certainly it was no intention of his that she should sacrifice her essential distinctiveness or feeling of nationhood. The cosmopolitanism that later in the century became for a time so marked in certain upper circles of Russian society was no true part of Peter's legacy; still less was the predominance of Baltic and other Germans under the empress Anna. He used foreigners to a far greater extent and in far larger numbers than his predecessors, recruiting them overhastily as and where he could from all layers of society, but he was always their master, using them to teach Russians, not to replace them.

Peter himself, though he consorted so much with foreigners, though he defied so many of the old traditional forms, was passionately devoted to Russia. With the exception of Lefort in the days of his youth, his closest companions were his own countrymen, not foreigners. The men he recruited from abroad were important—some of them indispensable—but in the main only as executants of his decisions and trainers of his cadres. This was especially so in the navy, the army, engineering, mining, industry, and education.

In the diplomatic service, which was in effect a new creation of Peter, foreigners gave way almost entirely to Russians in the major posts, while in the foreign office Osterman was the only foreigner to occupy a high position, and most of the subordinate personnel were Russians. It is important to realize that, despite the widespread contemporary hostility to the influx from abroad, Peter depended at all times upon Russians, not foreigners, for almost the whole of his governmental work. They alone worked his taxation system, filled the provincial governorships, and sat in the senate.

Just as in Russia the foreigners played mainly a rather narrow technical, training rôle, so, as has been emphasized earlier (p. 136), the Russians whom Peter sent to the West were assigned almost exclusively to technical training. This second aspect of his westernization, going to school in the West, was perhaps in its ultimate influence the most far-reaching of his innovations, but in his own lifetime it neither led to the results he desired nor had much immediate effect upon Russian culture. His own intensely practical bent and his coarse heavy-handedness caused him to treat his subjects far too much like inanimate objects upon which could be rapidly imposed a new impress or novel tasks. Most of the Russians sent abroad were from the upper class, and most of these, though there was a handful of notable exceptions, seem to have wasted their time and on return settled back into their old ways.

Within the next two generations, however, very different results began to flow from Peter's peremptory insistence on training abroad. Among many of the upper class a taste for foreign travel rapidly developed, once it was no longer obligatory and no longer to be spent in antipathetic apprenticeship to navigation or gunnery. From such travel, and from Peter's opening of the door to foreign books and foreign ideas, modern Russian literature and culture were born.

As would be expected of the soldier and sailor, the mechanic and the handicraftsman, Peter contributed little himself to literature or culture in the broad sense, but much to the furtherance of the exact sciences. With him arabic numerals, hitherto very little known, began to come into regular use. Logarithms made their first appearance, and Russia was introduced to the Copernican system. He was the founder of the first newspaper, a bleak, official journal; of the first public theatre, a troubled and insecure venture; of the first hospital, needless to say a military one, to which was attached something of a medical training school. He actively extended geographical knowledge and cartography, especially in Asia, and actively encouraged astronomy. If his schemes for education bore all the marks of the improviser whose main interests lay elsewhere, yet they jolted men towards new ideas and new knowledge, especially in mathematics and science, and in his dying bequest of the Academy of Sciences, which his wife opened in 1726, he laid the foundation of what was to become one of the greatest promoters of learning in Russia.

Characteristically, when he introduced a simplified fount in which all secular books were to be printed, he literally dotted the i's and crossed the t's of the new script, even though he had on his hands at the time all the weight of Charles XII's 1708 offensive. The new type was of considerable importance in emphasizing the growing cultural secularization which had indeed begun before his day, but was now so marked in the increase of nonreligious and of foreign books and in the developing taste for the western cult of classicism and for western romantic tales.

Ever since the time of "the great embassy," Peter took much trouble in extending printing, ordering translations, and encouraging the acquisition of foreign books and the formation of libraries. The printing presses belonged to the state or the church (there were no private presses until the last quarter of the eighteenth century), and their output was remarkable in quantity. Whereas in the whole of the seventeenth century only three hundred and seventy-four books were published, in the twenty-seven years following Peter's first journey to the West seven hundred publications appeared. In the former period a beggarly nineteen were secular books; under Peter almost four hundred. The contrast is immense, but it must be added that not far short of half of Peter's secular publications consisted of his edicts, manifestoes, jusifications of his policy and accounts of military operations. He was fully conscious of the need for propaganda both at home and abroad, and he was the first Russian sovereign to use the printing press for this purpose.

The other main use he made of the printing press was for military and naval manuals, but the share of general literature and history was diminutive. Even of this share a number (among them Æsop's fables, almost the only good seller, and Ovid's *Metamorphoses*) were already before his day known at least to a few in manuscript form. In the general field of the arts, there was no startling break with the past and few notable new contributions. For the average Russian the mainstay of what he or she read or heard read aloud was still as previously the Orthodox version of the Golden Legend, together with the newer tales of chivalry and romance that were filtering in through Poland. Both these continued to be staples far into the eighteenth century.

Modern Russian literature is to be dated from the reign of Elizabeth rather than of Peter; but it could not then have come into being had he not opened so many doors that previously had been closed or at least only ajar. But for the new opportunities created by him, the career of the remarkable polymath, Lomonosov (1711–65), would have been impossible; the son of a White Sea peasant farmer, who made himself almost equally famous in chemistry, literature, and history. There is an element of truth in the calculation made with mock-elaborate exactitude by one of Catherine the Great's grandees that without Peter it would have taken Russia until 1892 to reach the stage of civilization in fact attained by her towards the close of the eighteenth century.

Peter was above all a great man of action, not a thinker or a planner; he never evolved any clearly defined policy of westernization. It has been said of him that like Oliver Cromwell and Martin Luther "he goes farthest who knows not where he goes." He began with what lay to hand for immediate ends, seizing on whatever suited his inquisitive mind and impetuous temperament. In the end he grew to entertain broad views that amounted to an all-round renovation of Muscovy, but they were not shaped or rounded to any neat pattern. In the end he realized that his work was rough-and-ready, that there were far too few of his subjects as yet either desirous or capable of fulfilling the tasks he imposed upon them, and that his schemes, for instance in education, were lopsided and could not quickly produce satisfactory results.

When he finally decided to establish the long-mooted Academy of Sciences and included in the plan a university, he was criticized even by his admirers: "There is no one to learn, for without secondary schools this academy will merely cost a great deal of money and yet be useless," Peter replied, in words that sum up the greater part of his legacy: "I have to harvest big stooks, but I have no mill; and there is not enough water close by to build a water mill; but there is water enough at a distance; only I shall have no time to make a canal, for the length of my life is uncertain, and therefore I am building the mill first and have only given orders for the canal to be begun, which will the better force my successors to bring water to the completed mill."

Further Reading

FAR THE BEST treatment of Peter and his reign available in English is in Klyuchevsky's great *History of Russia,* vol. 4, pp. 1–264 (London; 1926), though the translation is bad and foreign affairs receive very little attention. On social, economic, and financial questions James Mavor's *An Economic History of Russia,* vol. 1, pp. 100–63 (London; 2nd edition; 1925), is informative.

There is no adequate biography of Peter. Much the most useful in English is the old-fashioned, solid work of an American student of Russia, E. Schuyler (2 vols; London; 1884). The biography by K. Waliszewski (London; 1897) should be used with caution. There are also biographies, all published in London, by Oscar Browning (1898), slight and second-hand but sensible, Stephen Graham (1929), and Georges Oudard (1930), shoddy and sensational.

In French, there is a valuable, and highly critical, analysis of Peter's reforms by Milyukov in *Histoire de Russie,* vol. 1, pp. 258–427 (Paris; 1932), edited by himself, C. Seignobos, and L. Eisenmann. Voltaire's *Histoire de Pierre le Grand* is full of interest.

In German, the second volume of Karl Stählin's *Geschichte Russlands,* pp. 1–190 (Berlin; 1930), contains an excellent account of Peter's life and reign. A. Brückner's biography (Berlin; 1879) is still useful as an introduction.

Alexis Tolstoi's novel *Peter the Great* (trans., London; 1936) is well worth reading. Pushkin's delightful novel *Peter the Great's Negro* is unfortunately only a brief fragment (trans. in *A Captain's Daughter and other Tales,* Everyman ed.). Part of his famous poem *Poltava* has been translated by B. Deutsch in *The Works of Alexander Pushkin* . . . , edited by A. Yarmolinsky (London; 1936). Merezhkovsky's remarkable novel on Peter, which follows closely good historical sources, is translated under the title *Peter and Alexis* (London; 1905).

The great bulk of the sources and literature on Peter the Great, upon which this book is based, is naturally in Russian. For these consult: *Istoriya S.S.S.R.,* ed. by V. I. Lebedev, B. D. Grekov, and S. V. Bakhrushin, vol. 1 (Moscow; 1939), pp. 777–8; M. N. Tikhomirov, *Istochnikovedenie istorii S.S.S.R.,* vol. 1, chaps. 16 to 20 (Moscow; 1940); S. R. Mintslov, *Obzor zapisok, dnevnikov, vospominanii . . .* pt. 1, pp. 69–84 (Novgorod; 1911); and B. Kafenhaus in *Istorichesky Zhurnal,* 1944, no. ix. Three works not mentioned in the above should be added: S. Platonov, *Peter Veliky* (Paris; 1927), a wayward sketch but by a great historian; M. M. Bogoslovsky, *Peter I: materialy dlya biografii* (5 vols., Moscow; 1940–8), an indispensable, posthumous publication of the very detailed researches of the greatest specialist on Peter, only reaching as far as 1700; E. I. Zaozerskaya, *Manufaktura pri Petre I* (Moscow; 1947). L. A. Nikiforov, *Russko-angliiske otnosheniya pri Petre I* (Moscow; 1950).

Contemporary foreign sources are valuable, but must be used with caution; see *e.g.* R. J. Kerner, *Slavic Europe; a Selected Bibliography in Western European Languages* (Harvard; 1918), pp. 33, 90–1. The reports from Russia of contemporary English, German, and French diplomats have been published in their original language by the Imperial Russian Historical Society; under that heading in the London Library catalogue there is a convenient list of them.

Index

Index

187